Steak au Poivre — P. 23 (R)

Casserole Cooking

Casserole Cooking

Jennie Reekie

OCTOPUS

First published 1976 by
Octopus Books Limited
59 Grosvenor Street, London W1

ISBN 7064 0535 8

Produced by Mandarin Publishers Limited
22A Westlands Road, Quarry Bay, Hong Kong

Printed in Hong Kong

Meat Casseroles
7

Different people have different ideas as to what constitutes a casserole dish, but in general, a casserole dish is one which is cooked in the oven and which, with a few exceptions, is served in the pot in which it has been cooked. The advantages of casseroling are legion: you can make use of the cheaper cuts of meat because the long, slow cooking not only tenderizes the meat, but also makes a dish which is full of flavour. Once put into the oven very few casseroles need any further attention before serving, so you can safely leave them to cook in the oven while you get on with other things, or you can go out of the house and leave them cooking. This type of dish is also very good for making full use of an automatic timer on an oven, but always remember to increase the cooking time by 30 minutes to allow for the oven to heat up. Not least of the advantages to a busy housewife is that casseroles reduce to a minimum the number of pots and pans to be washed up—surely one of the dreariest household tasks!

If you walk into the kitchen department of any large department store, or specialist kitchen shop, the enormous range of casserole pots that one can buy is almost unbelievable. There are hundreds of different sorts of rustic, earthenware pots, both glazed and unglazed, cast iron oven-to-tableware, enamelware, special glazed, heat-resistant dishes and elegant glazed pottery. This wide choice can sometimes be confusing, so before buying a dish it is best to look at several carefully and check whether they are flameproof (for use both on top of the stove and in the oven) or ovenproof only, whether they may have a tendency to chip and, lastly, how easy they are to clean. Always follow manufacturers' instructions on cleaning as you can ruin the surface of some pans by using scouring powders. If food does seem to be caked hard on to the sides of the pot, try soaking it in cold water as soon as you have finished using it. You will generally find that after a few hours it is quite easy to clean.

Contents

Meat Casseroles

A meat casserole of some sort probably provides the basis of one, if not more, meals a week in most households. They are among the most versatile dishes, ranging from a humble family 'stew' to a rather more exotic dish with wine, shallots, fresh herbs, etc. One of the many advantages of this type of dish is that it can be prepared in advance and reheated, which is of particular value when entertaining, both for busy housewives, working wives and bachelor girls. The flavour of many meat, poultry and game casseroles is often improved if they are prepared ahead of time because the cooling down and standing period allows the flavours of all the foods to become well infused. The casserole should be allowed to cool, then covered and put into a refrigerator or cold larder where it will keep for 2 to 3 days without deterioration, although greater care must be taken of dishes containing offal (variety meat).

Meat, poultry and game casseroles are also some of the most suitable cooked dishes for deep-freezing and all the recipes in this and the poultry and game chapter can be frozen unless stated otherwise. Any specific points for freezing a particular recipe are dealt with at the end of the recipe, but generally the casserole should be turned into a plastic or foil freezing container and cooled as quickly as possible, preferably by standing in a bowl of cold water. Cover tightly, then freeze. If you want to freeze a dish which is cooked in layers it is best to line your casserole with foil, freeze the food in the casserole, then take it out of the casserole in the foil. If you have sufficient time it is always best to allow the casserole to defrost completely before reheating, either in a refrigerator for about 24 hours or at room temperature for 8 to 12 hours. However, if you forget to take it out of the freezer or find you are suddenly faced with feeding six hungry people, you can place the frozen mass in a casserole and reheat it in a moderate oven, 180°C, 350°F, Gas Mark 4 for 1 to 1½ hours, depending on the quantity and type of casserole. Stir the casserole several times while it is reheating, if heating it from frozen.

Casseroles respond very well to the 'Eat one, freeze two or three' principle as it requires very little extra effort to cook a casserole for 12 than it does for four. But always remember to label items clearly before you put them into the freezer—a frozen hunk of stew is one of the most difficult things to identify!

Topside (Top Round) Slices with Red Wine

METRIC/IMPERIAL

4 slices of beef topside, cut 1.25 cm./½ in. thick
125 ml./¼ pint red wine
1 onion, chopped
1 bay leaf
1 parsley sprig
1 thyme sprig
1 marjoram sprig
25 g./1 oz. beef dripping
25 g./1 oz. flour
250 ml./½ pint beef stock
salt and freshly ground black pepper
200 g./8 oz. carrots, sliced
200 g./8 oz. button onions
1 tablespoon chopped parsley

AMERICAN

4 slices of beef top round, cut ½ in. thick
⅝ cup red wine
1 onion, chopped
1 bay leaf
1 parsley sprig
1 thyme sprig
1 marjoram sprig
2 tablespoons beef dripping
¼ cup flour
1¼ cups beef stock
salt and freshly ground black pepper
8 oz. carrots, sliced
8 oz. button onions
1 tablespoon chopped parsley

Lay the beef slices in a shallow dish. Pour over the wine and add the onion and herbs. Leave to marinate in a cool place for 5 to 6 hours, turning occasionally.

Drain the meat and strain and reserve the marinade. Melt the dripping in a large pan, add the meat and cook on both sides until brown. Remove from the pan and place in a casserole. Add the flour to the fat remaining in the pan and cook over a low heat until the flour is browned, but not burnt. Stir in the stock and reserved marinade and bring to the boil, stirring all the time. Season and pour over the meat in the casserole. Cover and cook in a cool oven, 150°C, 300°F, Gas Mark 2, for 1½ hours.

Add the carrots and onions to the casserole and cook for a further 1 hour. Taste and adjust the seasoning and sprinkle with chopped parsley. **Serves 4**

Boeuf Bourguignonne

Made up in a larger quantity and served with boiled rice and a tossed salad this is a good buffet party dish.

METRIC/IMPERIAL
25 g./1 oz. bacon fat or pork dripping
150 g./6 oz. fat bacon or salt pork, cut into cubes
600 g./1½ lb. chuck or buttock steak, cubed
15 g./½ oz. flour
250 ml./½ pint beef stock
125 ml./¼ pint red wine (this should be a Burgundy, but any full bodied wine can be used)
1 bay leaf
1 thyme sprig
1 parsley sprig
salt and black pepper
100 g./4 oz. button onions
100 g./4 oz. button mushrooms
4 carrots, sliced
2 tablespoons chopped parsley

AMERICAN
2 tablespoons bacon fat or pork dripping
6 oz. fat bacon or salt pork, cubed
1½ lb. chuck or buttock steak, cut into cubes
2 tablespoons flour
1¼ cups beef stock
⅝ cup red wine (this should be a Burgundy, but any full bodied wine can be used)
1 bay leaf
1 thyme sprig
1 parsley sprig
salt and black pepper
4 oz. button onions
4 oz. button mushrooms
4 carrots, sliced
2 tablespoons chopped parsley

Melt the bacon fat or pork dripping in a large pan and fry the bacon or pork over a moderate heat for about 10 minutes. Remove from the pan with a slotted spoon and put into a casserole. Fry the steak in the fat remaining in the pan until browned on all sides. Remove from the pan and put into the casserole with the bacon or pork.

Blend the flour with the fat remaining in the pan and cook over a gentle heat until the flour is browned, but not burnt. Gradually stir in the stock and wine and bring to the boil, stirring all the time. Pour over the meat and bacon in the casserole and add the herbs and seasoning. Cover and cook in a warm oven, 170°C, 325°F, Gas Mark 3 for 1½ hours. Add the onions, mushrooms and carrots and continue cooking for a further 1 hour. Taste and adjust the seasoning, skim off any fat from the surface and remove the herbs. Sprinkle with parsley just before serving.

Serves 6

Stufato di Manzo ►

This is an interesting beef casserole from Italy.

METRIC/IMPERIAL	AMERICAN
1 teaspoon salt	*1 teaspoon salt*
freshly ground black pepper	*freshly ground black pepper*
1 bay leaf, crushed	*1 bay leaf, crushed*
2 teaspoons chopped fresh thyme	*2 teaspoons chopped fresh thyme*
2 medium-sized onions, chopped	*2 medium-sized onions, chopped*
2 garlic cloves, crushed	*2 garlic cloves, crushed*
3 celery stalks, chopped	*3 celery stalks, chopped*
250 ml./½ pint red wine	*1¼ cups red wine*
1 kg./2½ lb. chuck steak, cut into cubes	*2½ lb. chuck steak, cut into cubes*
1 tablespoon olive oil	*1 tablespoon olive oil*
4 bacon rashers, chopped	*4 bacon slices, chopped*
2 tablespoons tomato purée	*2 tablespoons tomato purée*
250 ml./½ pint beef stock	*1¼ cups beef stock*
1 tablespoon chopped parsley	*1 tablespoon chopped parsley*

Put the salt, pepper, bay leaf, thyme, 1 onion, the garlic, 1 celery stalk and the wine into a bowl. Mix together, then add the cubes of meat. Cover and leave to marinate in a cool place for 5 to 6 hours, turning occasionally.

Drain the meat well and strain and reserve the marinade. Heat the oil in a flameproof casserole. Add the remaining onion and celery and the bacon and fry gently until soft and pale golden. Add the beef cubes and fry fairly quickly until browned on all sides. Add the reserved marinade, tomato purée and stock. Cover and cook in a cool oven, 150°C, 300°F, Gas Mark 2 for 2½ hours. Taste and adjust the seasoning before serving sprinkled with parsley. **Serves 6**

Salt Brisket (Corned Beef) Casserole

METRIC/IMPERIAL	AMERICAN
800 g./2 lb. salt brisket	*2 lb. corned beef*
2 onions, chopped	*2 onions, chopped*
4 carrots, sliced	*4 carrots, sliced*
1 turnip, chopped	*1 turnip, chopped*
500 ml./1 pint water	*2½ cups water*
salt and pepper	*salt and pepper*
25 g./1 oz. flour	*¼ cup flour*
200 g./8 oz. peas	*8 oz. peas*

Soak the brisket (beef) overnight in cold water and drain. Cut into cubes, removing some of the excess fat, and put into a casserole with the onions, carrots, turnip, water and seasoning. Cover and cook in a warm oven, 170°C, 325°F, Gas Mark 3 for 3½ hours.

Blend the flour to a smooth paste with some of the liquid in the casserole. Add to the casserole a teaspoon at a time, stirring well, then stir in the peas. Return to the oven and cook for a further 30 minutes. Stir the casserole and taste and adjust the seasoning before serving. **Serves 4 to 6**

Marinated Beef Casserole

METRIC/IMPERIAL	AMERICAN
4 onions, sliced	*4 onions, sliced*
2 carrots, sliced	*2 carrots, sliced*
2 garlic gloves, crushed	*2 garlic cloves, crushed*
1 bay leaf	*1 bay leaf*
1 rosemary sprig	*1 rosemary sprig*
3 parsley sprigs	*3 parsley sprigs*
2 cloves	*2 cloves*
salt and pepper	*salt and pepper*
thinly pared rind of ½ orange	*thinly pared rind of ½ orange*
375 ml./¾ pint red wine	*2 cups red wine*
800 g./2 lb. good quality braising steak, cut into cubes	*2 lb. good quality braising steak, cut into cubes*
2 thick streaky bacon rashers, chopped	*2 thick fatty bacon slices, chopped*
25 g./1 oz. flour	*¼ cup flour*

Put two onions and the remaining ingredients except the meat, bacon and flour into a shallow dish. Add the beef cubes and leave to marinate for 12 to 24 hours, turning occasionally.

Drain the meat from the marinade and reserve the marinade. Fry the bacon gently in a flameproof casserole until the fat runs. Add the drained meat and remaining onions and cook for 10 minutes or until the meat is browned on all sides. Stir in the flour and cook over a very gentle heat until lightly browned, stirring frequently. Gradually stir in the strained marinade and bring to the boil, stirring all the time. Cover and cook in a cool oven, 150°C, 300°F, Gas Mark 2 for 4 hours. Remove any excess fat from the surface and taste and adjust the seasoning before serving. **Serves 4 to 6**

Ragoût of Beef and Prunes

METRIC/IMPERIAL
500 g./$1\frac{1}{4}$ lb. stewing steak, cut into $2\frac{1}{2}$ cm./1 in. pieces
25 g./1 oz. dripping
25 g./1 oz. flour
375 ml./$\frac{3}{4}$ pint stock, or water and 1 beef stock cube
425 g./15 oz. can tomatoes
200 g./8 oz. tenderized prunes
salt and pepper

AMERICAN
$1\frac{1}{4}$ lb. stewing steak, cut into 1 in. pieces
2 tablespoons dripping
$\frac{1}{4}$ cup flour
2 cups stock, or water and 1 beef stock cube
15 oz. can tomatoes
8 oz. tenderized prunes
salt and pepper

Fry the steak pieces in the dripping in a flameproof casserole or pan for 5 minutes. Sprinkle over the flour and cook over a very gentle heat for about 5 minutes or until the flour is lightly browned. Gradually stir in the stock or water and stock cube and bring to the boil, stirring all the time. Add the tomatoes, with the juice from the can, the prunes and seasoning. If cooking in a pan, turn into a casserole. Cover and cook in a warm oven, 170°C, 325°F, Gas Mark 3 for $2\frac{1}{2}$ hours. Taste and adjust the seasoning before serving. **Serves 4**

Note: *If not using tenderized prunes (which require no soaking), soak the prunes overnight in cold water, then drain. Reduce the stock or water to 250 ml./$\frac{1}{2}$ pint ($1\frac{1}{4}$ cups).*

Rich Beef Casserole with Mustard Croûtes

METRIC/IMPERIAL
600 g./1½ lb. stewing steak
2 tablespoons oil
1 large onion, chopped
1 tablespoon flour
250 ml./½ pint light ale
1 tablespoon French mustard
1 tablespoon tomato purée
50 g./2 oz. seedless raisins
salt and pepper

For the mustard croûtes:
2 slices white bread
1 teaspoon dry mustard
oil for frying
1 tablespoon chopped parsley

AMERICAN
1½ lb. stewing steak
2 tablespoons oil
1 large onion, chopped
1 tablespoon flour
1¼ cups light ale
1 tablespoon French mustard
1 tablespoon tomato purée
⅓ cup seedless raisins
salt and pepper

For the mustard croûtes:
2 slices white bread
1 teaspoon dry mustard
oil for frying
1 tablespoon chopped parsley

Cut the beef into 3¾ cm./1½ in. cubes. Heat the oil in a frying pan and quickly brown the meat on all sides. Remove from the pan with a slotted spoon and place in a casserole. Add the onion to the pan and cook gently for 5 minutes. Sprinkle over the flour and cook for a further 8 minutes, stirring frequently, until the flour is pale golden. Remove from the heat and stir in the light ale. Return to the heat and bring to the boil, stirring all the time until thickened. Add the mustard, tomato purée, raisins and seasoning and pour into the casserole. Cover and cook in a warm oven, 170°C, 325°F, Gas Mark 3 for 2½ hours. Taste and adjust the seasoning before serving.

For the croûtes, cut the crusts off the bread and cut the bread into small triangles. Place in a shallow bowl and sift the mustard over them. Shake the bowl gently to coat the bread. Fry in hot oil on both sides until golden brown. Drain well and sprinkle with parsley. Serve the casserole garnished with the mustard croûtes.

Serves 4

Note: *Do not deep freeze the croûtes.*

Beef Olives

METRIC/IMPERIAL
4 slices beef topside
3 onions
200 g./8 oz. ox kidney, finely chopped
1 tablespoon chopped parsley
1 teaspoon chopped fresh thyme
25 g./1 oz. butter, melted
salt and pepper
25 g./1 oz. flour
25 g./1 oz. dripping
6 large carrots, sliced
250 ml./½ pint stock

To garnish:
2 tablespoons chopped parsley

AMERICAN
4 slices top round steak
3 onions
8 oz. ox kidney, finely chopped
1 tablespoon chopped parsley
1 teaspoon chopped fresh thyme
2 tablespoons butter, melted
salt and pepper
¼ cup flour
2 tablespoons dripping
6 large carrots, sliced
1¼ cups stock

To garnish:
2 tablespoons chopped parsley

Cut the slices of beef in half, place between two sheets of greaseproof (waxed) paper and bat out, using a rolling pin or meat mallet. Finely chop one onion and mix together with the kidney, parsley, thyme, melted butter and seasoning. Divide this mixture between the eight slices of meat. Roll the meat up tightly and secure with fine string or coarse thread. Coat the meat rolls with the flour, seasoned with salt and pepper.

Melt the dripping in a large pan and fry the meat rolls on all sides until golden brown. Remove from the pan and put on a plate on one side. Slice the remaining two onions and fry in the fat remaining in the pan with the carrots for about 5 minutes. Add the stock and bring to the boil. Transfer to a casserole. Place the beef rolls on top, together with any meat juices from the plate, and cover the casserole. Cook in a warm oven, 170°C, 325°F, Gas Mark 3 for 2 hours. Serve sprinkled with parsley.

Serves 4

Locro de Trigo

A recipe from the Argentine, this is rather like a very thick soup and makes a complete meal with French bread.

METRIC/IMPERIAL
2 tablespoons oil
2 onions, chopped
1 red pepper, seeded and diced
600 g./1½ lb. stewing steak, finely diced
2 teaspoons paprika
1 l./2 pints brown stock, or water and 2 beef stock cubes
3 streaky bacon rashers, chopped
200 g./8 oz. red or garlic sausage, sliced
100 g./4 oz. dried butter beans, soaked overnight and drained
198 g./7 oz. can sweetcorn, drained
salt and pepper

AMERICAN
2 tablespoons oil
2 onions, chopped
1 red pepper, seeded and diced
1½ lb. stewing steak, finely diced
2 teaspoons paprika
5 cups brown stock, or water and 2 beef stock cubes
3 fatty bacon slices, chopped
8 oz. red or garlic sausage, sliced
⅔ cup dried butter beans, soaked overnight and drained
7 oz. can sweetcorn, drained
salt and pepper

Heat the oil in a large pan and fry the onions, pepper and beef for 5 minutes. Add the paprika, then the stock or water and stock cubes. Add the bacon and sausage to the pan with the beans. Turn into a casserole, cover and cook in a cool oven, 150°C, 300°F, Gas Mark 2 for 2½ hours. Add the corn and cook for a further 30 minutes. Taste and adjust the seasoning before serving. **Serves 6**

Lasagne al forno ►

METRIC/IMPERIAL
For the meat sauce:
2 tablespoons oil
2 bacon rashers, chopped
200 g./8 oz. minced beef
1 large onion, chopped
2 celery stalks, chopped
1 garlic clove, crushed
pinch of dried mixed herbs
salt and black pepper
pinch of sugar
70 g./2¼ oz. can tomato purée
125 ml./¼ pint water

For the béchamel sauce:
300 ml./generous ½ pint milk
1 small bay leaf
½ small onion
1 piece carrot
1 piece celery
4 peppercorns
25 g./1 oz. butter
25 g./1 oz. flour
salt and pepper

For the lasagne:
salt
1 tablespoon oil
150 g./6 oz. lasagne pasta, plain or green
75 g./3 oz. Gruyère or Emmenthal cheese, grated
25 g./1 oz. Parmesan cheese, grated

AMERICAN
For the meat sauce:
2 tablespoons oil
2 bacon slices, chopped
8 oz. ground beef
1 large onion, chopped
2 celery stalks, chopped
1 garlic clove, crushed
pinch of dried mixed herbs
salt and black pepper
pinch of sugar
2¼ oz. can tomato purée
⅝ cup water

For the béchamel sauce:
1½ cups milk
1 small bay leaf
½ small onion
1 piece carrot
1 piece celery
4 peppercorns
2 tablespoons butter
¼ cup flour
salt and pepper

For the lasagne:
salt
1 tablespoon oil
6 oz. lasagne pasta, plain or green
¾ cup grated Gruyère or Emmenthal cheese
¼ cup grated Parmesan cheese

To prepare the meat sauce, put the oil into a pan and slowly fry the bacon, beef and onion until browned, stirring frequently. Add the celery, garlic, herbs, seasoning, sugar, tomato purée and water. Cover and simmer gently for about 1 hour, stirring occasionally.

To prepare the béchamel sauce, pour the milk into a saucepan. Add the bay leaf, onion, carrot, celery and peppercorns and bring slowly to simmering point.Remove from the heat and leave the milk for 20 to 30 minutes to infuse. In a clean pan, melt the butter, add the flour and cook for 1 minute. Gradually stir in the strained milk and bring to the boil, stirring all the time. Remove from the heat and add seasoning to taste.

Bring a large pan of salted water to the boil, add the oil, then add the lasagne piece by piece. Boil for about 8 minutes or until barely tender, then drain and rinse in cold water. Lay the lasagne out flat on a clean, damp cloth to dry; this prevents the pieces from sticking together.

To assemble, put half the meat sauce in the bottom of an ovenproof dish, cover with half the pasta, then half the béchamel sauce and sprinkle with most of the grated Gruyère or Emmenthal cheese. Repeat these layers, finishing with the sauce. (If you wish you can put a few tablespoons of the meat sauce on the top as in the photograph.) Mix the remaining Gruyère or Emmenthal cheese with the Parmesan and sprinkle over the top. Cook in a moderately hot oven, 190°C, 375°F, Gas Mark 5 for 30 minutes or until the top is golden brown. **Serves 4**

Note: *Made up in a larger quantity than given here, this recipe is particularly suitable for a buffet party as it is easy to eat with a fork and can be pre-prepared or deep frozen in advance.*

Winter Casserole

METRIC/IMPERIAL
4 tablespoons Worcestershire sauce
300 ml./½ pint plus 4 tablespoons water
1 teaspoon salt
600 g./1½ lb. shin of beef, cut into cubes
25 g./1 oz. dripping
4 large carrots, sliced
2 leeks, sliced
200 g./8 oz. swede, cut in cubes
50 g./2 oz. flour
250 ml./½ pint brown ale
pepper
425 g./15 oz. can butter beans, drained

AMERICAN
4 tablespoons Worcestershire sauce
1¼ cups plus 4 tablespoons water
1 teaspoon salt
1½ lb. shank end of beef, cut into cubes
2 tablespoons dripping
4 large carrots, sliced
2 leeks, sliced
8 oz. rutabaga, cut in cubes
½ cup flour
1¼ cups brown ale
pepper
15 oz. can butter beans, drained

Mix together the Worcestershire sauce, 4 tablespoons of the water and the salt. Put the beef cubes in a shallow dish. Pour over the Worcestershire sauce mixture and leave to marinate in the refrigerator for 4 hours, or overnight, turning occasionally. Drain the meat and reserve the marinade.

Heat the dripping in a frying pan and brown the meat on all sides. Remove from the pan with a slotted spoon and place in a casserole. Add all the vegetables, except the beans, to the frying pan and cook gently for 5 minutes. Blend in the flour. Remove from the heat and gradually stir in the remaining water, the ale, reserved marinade and pepper. Return to the heat and bring to the boil, stirring. Pour into the casserole, stir, cover and cook in a warm oven, 170°C, 325°F, Gas Mark 3 for 2 hours. Add the butter beans and cook for a further 1 hour. Taste and adjust the seasoning before serving. **Serves 4 to 6**

Slimmers' Beef Casserole ►

METRIC/IMPERIAL	AMERICAN
400 g./1 lb. lean, good quality braising steak	*1 lb. lean, good quality braising steak*
salt and pepper	*salt and pepper*
400 g./1 lb. tomatoes, peeled and quartered	*1 lb. tomatoes, peeled and quartered*
1 green pepper, seeded and chopped	*1 green pepper, seeded and chopped*
1 large onion, chopped	*1 large onion, chopped*
3 celery stalks, chopped	*3 celery stalks, chopped*
1 tablespoon Worcestershire sauce	*1 tablespoon Worcestershire sauce*

Trim off all the excess fat from the steak. Season well with salt and pepper. Put under a hot grill (broiler) for about 5 minutes, then turn and grill (broil) for a further 5 minutes on the other side to seal in the meat juices. Place in a large, shallow casserole with the tomatoes, green pepper, onion, celery, Worcestershire sauce and seasoning. Cover tightly and cook in a warm oven, 170°C, 325°F, Gas Mark 3 for 3 hours.

Serves 4

Braised Beef

METRIC/IMPERIAL	AMERICAN
800 g./2 lb. boned and rolled brisket of beef	*2 lb. boned and rolled brisket of beef*
1 tablespoon flour	*1 tablespoon flour*
salt and pepper	*salt and pepper*
25 g./1 oz. dripping	*2 tablespoons dripping*
2 onions, sliced	*2 onions, sliced*
2 carrots, sliced	*2 carrots, sliced*
1 small turnip, peeled and sliced	*1 small turnip, peeled and sliced*
250 ml./½ pint stock or water	*1¼ cups stock or water*
1 bouquet garni	*1 bouquet garni*

Coat the meat with the flour, seasoned with salt and pepper. Heat the dripping in a large flameproof casserole and fry the meat on all sides until well browned. Remove from the pan and place on a plate. Add the onions, carrots and turnip to the fat remaining in the casserole and fry for about 10 minutes or until lightly browned. Replace the meat, pour over the stock or water and add the bouquet garni and seasoning. Cover and cook in a cool oven, 150°C, 300°F, Gas Mark 2 for 2 hours. Taste and adjust the seasoning and remove the bouquet garni before serving.

Serves 6

Note: *If wished, the juice from cooking the meat can be thickened by adding 1 tablespoon of cornflour (cornstarch) dissolved in 1 tablespoon of water. Bring to the boil and cook for 2 to 3 minutes until thickened.*

Country Beef Casserole ►

METRIC/IMPERIAL	AMERICAN
600 g./1½ lb. shin of beef	*1½ lb. shank end of beef*
1 tablespoon oil	*1 tablespoon oil*
15 g./½ oz. butter	*1 tablespoon butter*
3 carrots, thinly sliced	*3 carrots, thinly sliced*
1 onion, cut into eighths	*1 onion, cut into eighths*
2 celery stalks, chopped	*2 celery stalks, chopped*
1 garlic clove, crushed	*1 garlic clove, crushed*
15 g./½ oz. flour	*2 tablespoons flour*
125 ml./¼ pint dry white wine or cider	*⅝ cup dry white wine or cider*
250 ml./½ pint stock	*1¼ cups stock*
425 g./15 oz. can tomatoes	*15 oz. can tomatoes*
1 parsley sprig	*1 parsley sprig*
1 bay leaf	*1 bay leaf*
salt and pepper	*salt and pepper*
8 stuffed green olives, sliced	*8 stuffed green olives, sliced*

Trim the beef and cut into 3¾ cm./1½ in. thick pieces. Heat the oil and butter in a large frying pan and fry half the meat at a time over a moderate heat, turning once, until browned. Remove from the pan with a slotted spoon and place in a casserole. Add the vegetables and garlic to the pan and fry for 5 minutes. Sprinkle the flour over the vegetables and continue to cook, stirring constantly, until the flour is golden brown. Gradually stir in the wine or cider, stock and tomatoes, together with the juice from the can. Bring to the boil, stirring all the time. Add the parsley, bay leaf and seasoning, and pour into the casserole.

Cover the casserole and cook in a warm oven, 170°C, 325°F, Gas Mark 3 for about 2½ hours or until the beef is tender. Remove the parsley and bay leaf. Taste and adjust the seasoning, then stir in the olives. **Serves 4 to 6**

Thatched Beefburgers and Beans

METRIC/IMPERIAL	AMERICAN
25 g./1 oz. butter	*2 tablespoons butter*
1 onion, chopped	*1 onion, chopped*
2 celery stalks, chopped	*2 celery stalks, chopped*
425 g./15 oz. can baked beans	*15 oz. can baked beans*
4 to 6 frozen beefburgers	*4 to 6 frozen beefburgers*
pinch of dried mixed herbs	*pinch of dried mixed herbs*
50 g./2 oz. Cheddar cheese, grated	*½ cup grated Cheddar cheese*

Melt the butter in a flameproof casserole and fry the onion and celery for 5 minutes. Remove from the heat and spoon the baked beans on top. Cover with the beefburgers and sprinkle with the herbs and cheese. Cover and cook in a moderate oven, 180°C, 350°F, Gas Mark 4 for 45 minutes. Remove the lid and cook uncovered for a further 15 minutes.

Serves 2 to 3

Cholent

This is a traditional Jewish dish which is made on Friday night to serve on the Sabbath.

METRIC/IMPERIAL	AMERICAN
200 g./8 oz. haricot or butter beans	*1⅓ cups haricot (dried white) or butter beans*
800 g./2 lb. fresh brisket or short rib of beef	*2 lb. fresh brisket or short rib of beef*
1 onion, chopped	*1 onion, chopped*
800 g./2 lb. potatoes, sliced	*2 lb. potatoes, sliced*
salt and pepper	*salt and pepper*
1 l./2 pints boiling water	*5 cups boiling water*
For the dumpling:	For the dumpling:
100 g./4 oz. self-raising flour	*1 cup self-rising flour*
salt and pepper	*salt and pepper*
25 g./1 oz. shredded suet	*⅛ cup shredded suet*
1 tablespoon finely chopped or grated onion	*1 tablespoon finely chopped or grated onion*
1 tablespoon chopped parsley	*1 tablespoon chopped parsley*
1 medium-sized potato, grated	*1 medium-sized potato, grated*
about 4 tablespoons cold water	*about 4 tablespoons cold water*

Place the beans in a large casserole; there is no need to soak the beans as the long slow cooking makes them very tender. Place the beef in the middle. Add the onion, mixed with the potatoes, leaving enough space for the dumpling to fit in. Season well with salt and pepper.

Sift the flour for the dumpling with salt and pepper. Add the suet, onion, parsley and potato and bind together with the cold water to form a soft but not sticky dough. On a lightly floured surface, form the dough into a roll and place in a lightly floured piece of muslin (cheesecloth). Tie loosely with string, to allow for the dumpling to expand, and place in the casserole. Pour over the boiling water, cover and cook in a moderately hot oven, 200°C, 400°F, Gas Mark 6 for 1½ hours, then lower the heat to 90°C, 175°F, Gas Mark ¼ and leave to cook overnight for lunch the following day. **Serves 4 to 6**

Steak and Kidney with Button Onions

METRIC/IMPERIAL
15 g./½ oz. butter
1 tablespoon oil
400 g./1 lb. button onions
600 g./1½ lb. steak and kidney
25 g./1 oz. flour
salt and pepper
500 ml./1 pint beef stock
1 thyme sprig
thinly pared rind of ½ small orange
2 tablespoons chopped parsley

AMERICAN
1 tablespoon butter
1 tablespoon oil
1 lb. button onions
1 lb. stewing steak, cubed
½ lb. kidney, quartered
¼ cup flour
salt and pepper
2½ cups beef stock
1 thyme sprig
thinly pared rind of ½ small orange
2 tablespoons chopped parsley

Heat the butter and oil in a flameproof casserole. Add the onions and cook for about 8 minutes or until they are golden brown. Coat the steak and kidney with the flour, seasoned with salt and pepper. Add to the casserole and fry for a further 5 minutes. Gradually stir in the stock and bring to the boil, stirring all the time. Add the thyme and orange rind, cover the casserole and cook in a moderate oven, 180°C, 350°F, Gas Mark 4 for 2 hours or until the meat is tender. Remove the thyme and orange rind and sprinkle with the chopped parsley before serving. **Serves 4 to 6**

Savoury Minced (Ground) Beef

METRIC/IMPERIAL
400 g./1 lb. minced beef
1 large onion, chopped
1 green pepper, seeded and chopped
1 garlic clove, crushed
1 tablespoon flour
226 g./8 oz. can tomatoes
220 g./7¾ oz. can baked beans
1 tablespoon tomato purée
salt and pepper
pinch of dried mixed herbs

AMERICAN
1 lb. ground beef
1 large onion, chopped
1 green pepper, seeded and chopped
1 garlic clove, crushed
1 tablespoon flour
8 oz. can tomatoes
7¾ oz. can baked beans
1 tablespoon tomato purée
salt and pepper
pinch of dried mixed herbs

Fry the beef in a flameproof casserole without any fat for 5 minutes or until browned. Add the onion, green pepper and garlic and fry for a further 5 to 10 minutes. Stir in the flour and cook for 1 minute, then add the tomatoes, with the juice from the can, the baked beans, tomato purée, seasoning and herbs. Stir well. Cover and cook in a moderate oven, 180°C, 350°F, Gas Mark 4 for 1 hour. **Serves 4**

Note: *If you want to, you can turn this delicious mixture into a Shepherd's Pie. Halfway through cooking, simply spread 400 g./1 lb. soft, mashed potato over the top and bake for the remaining time uncovered.*

Chilli con Carne

METRIC/IMPERIAL
2 tablespoons oil
1 large onion, chopped
2 garlic cloves, crushed
1 green pepper, seeded and chopped
100 g./4 oz. streaky bacon, chopped
400 g./1 lb. minced beef
425 g./15 oz. can tomatoes
425 g./15 oz. can red kidney beans, drained
4 teaspoons chilli powder
salt

AMERICAN
2 tablespoons oil
1 large onion, chopped
2 garlic cloves, crushed
1 green pepper, seeded and chopped
4 oz. fatty bacon, chopped
1 lb. ground beef
15 oz. can tomatoes
15 oz. can red kidney beans, drained
4 teaspoons chilli powder
salt

Heat the oil in a flameproof casserole and fry the onion, garlic, green pepper and bacon for 5 minutes. Add the beef, stir well and fry for a further 5 minutes. Add the remaining ingredients and blend well. Cover and cook in a warm oven, 170°C, 325°F, Gas Mark 3 for 1 hour. Taste and adjust the seasoning before serving. **Serves 4**

Note: *Chilli powder can vary considerably in strength – some brands are quite mild, but others are very strong and ½ to 1 teaspoon of these would be plenty.*

Casseroled Steak au Poivre

The flavour of the traditional fried steak is retained in this casserole, but a cheaper cut of meat is used.

METRIC/IMPERIAL
300g./12 oz. lean buttock steak, cut in one piece $1\frac{1}{4}$ to $2\frac{1}{2}$ cm./$\frac{1}{2}$ to 1 in. thick or 2 thick slices of topside
2 to 3 teaspoons black peppercorns
salt
25 g./1 oz. butter
1 tablespoon olive oil
4 tablespoons red wine
4 medium-sized courgettes, thickly sliced
3 tomatoes, quartered

AMERICAN
2 thick slices of top round
2 to 3 teaspoons black peppercorns
salt
2 tablespoons butter
1 tablespoon olive oil
4 tablespoons red wine
4 medium-sized zucchini, thickly sliced
3 tomatoes, quartered

If using buttock steak, cut the piece in half to give two steaks. Crush the peppercorns either with a pestle and mortar or with a rolling pin on a board. Press the crushed peppercorns into both sides of the steak and season with a little salt as well. Heat the butter and oil in a large frying pan and fry the steaks quickly on each side for 3 to 4 minutes, then remove from the pan and place in a casserole. Mix the red wine with the pan juices and boil rapidly for 2 to 3 minutes. Pour over the steaks in the casserole. Cover and cook in a warm oven, 170°C, 325 °F, Gas Mark 3 for 1 hour. Add the courgettes (zucchini) and tomatoes to the casserole and cook for a further 1 hour.

Serves 2

◄

Family Beef and Mushroom Casserole

METRIC/IMPERIAL	AMERICAN
400 g./1 lb. stewing steak	*1 lb. stewing steak*
25 g./1 oz. cornflour	*$\frac{1}{4}$ cup cornstarch*
salt and pepper	*salt and pepper*
2 tablespoons oil	*2 tablespoons oil*
200 g./8 oz. button onions	*8 oz. button onions*
1 garlic clove, crushed	*1 garlic clove, crushed*
2 carrots, sliced	*2 carrots, sliced*
2 beef stock cubes	*2 beef stock cubes*
500 ml./1 pint water	*$2\frac{1}{2}$ cups water*
50 g./2 oz. mushrooms, sliced	*2 oz. mushrooms, sliced*
10 black olives	*10 black olives*

Trim off any excess fat and gristle from the meat and cut into cubes. Coat with the cornflour (cornstarch), seasoned with salt and pepper. Heat the oil in a flameproof casserole and lightly fry the meat, onions and garlic for 10 minutes. Add the carrots, beef stock cubes and water and bring to the boil, stirring all the time. Cover and cook in a warm oven, 170°C, 325°F, Gas Mark 3 for 2 hours. Add the mushrooms and olives and cook for a further 30 minutes or until the meat is tender. Taste and adjust the seasoning before serving.

Serves 4

Beef Carbonnade

METRIC/IMPERIAL	AMERICAN
600 g./$1\frac{1}{2}$ lb. stewing steak	*$1\frac{1}{2}$ lb. stewing steak*
25 g./1 oz. lard or dripping	*2 tablespoons lard or dripping*
2 large onions, chopped	*2 large onions, chopped*
25 g./1 oz. flour	*$\frac{1}{4}$ cup flour*
250 ml./$\frac{1}{2}$ pint light ale	*$1\frac{1}{4}$ cups light ale*
125 ml./$\frac{1}{4}$ pint water	*$\frac{5}{8}$ cup water*
$\frac{1}{4}$ teaspoon dried thyme	*$\frac{1}{4}$ teaspoon dried thyme*
1 bay leaf	*1 bay leaf*
1 teaspoon sugar	*1 teaspoon sugar*
salt and pepper	*salt and pepper*

Cut the beef into $3\frac{3}{4}$ cm./$1\frac{1}{2}$ in. cubes. Heat the lard or dripping in a large frying pan and brown the meat quickly on all sides. Remove the meat from the pan with a slotted spoon and place in a casserole. Add the onions to the pan and fry until golden. Blend in the flour and cook for 2 minutes, stirring. Gradually stir in the ale and water and bring to the boil, stirring all the time. Pour into the casserole and add the thyme, bay leaf, sugar and seasoning. Cover and cook in a moderate oven, 180°C, 350°F, Gas Mark 4 for about 2 hours or until the meat is tender. Taste and adjust the seasoning and remove the bay leaf before serving.

Serves 4

Hungarian Goulash ►

METRIC/IMPERIAL	AMERICAN
¾ kg./1½ lb. good quality stewing beef	*1½ lb. good quality stewing beef*
25 g./1 oz. flour	*¼ cup flour*
1 teaspoon salt	*1 teaspoon salt*
1½ tablespoons paprika	*1½ tablespoons paprika*
25 g./1 oz. dripping	*2 tablespoons dripping*
1 large onion, chopped	*1 large onion, chopped*
½ kg./1 lb. tomatoes, peeled and quartered	*1 lb. tomatoes, peeled and quartered*
375 ml./¾ pint beef stock	*2 cups beef stock*
1 teaspoon caraway seeds (optional)	*1 teaspoon caraway seeds (optional)*
½ kg./1 lb. potatoes, sliced	*1 lb. potatoes, sliced*
125 ml./¼ pint soured cream	*⅝ cup sour cream*

Cut the beef into 3¾ cm./1½ in. cubes and coat with the flour, seasoned with salt and paprika. Melt the dripping in a flameproof casserole, add the onion and fry for a few minutes. Add the meat and cook for a further 5 minutes, stirring until the meat is evenly browned. Add the tomatoes and gradually stir in the stock. Bring to the boil, stirring all the time. Add the caraway seeds, if using, and the potatoes, cover the casserole and cook in a warm oven, 170°C, 325°F, Gas Mark 3 for 2½ hours. Remove the casserole from the oven, allow to cool slightly, then stir in the soured cream. **Serves 4**

Note: *If wishing to deep freeze this dish, do not add the cream before freezing. Reheat and stir in the cream just before serving.*

Potato Burger Pie

METRIC/IMPERIAL	AMERICAN
400 g./1 lb. potatoes, grated	*1 lb. potatoes, grated*
400 g./1 lb. minced beef	*1 lb. ground beef*
1 large onion, grated	*1 large onion, grated*
226 g./8 oz. can tomatoes	*8 oz. can tomatoes*
2 tablespoons chopped parsley	*2 tablespoons chopped parsley*
salt and pepper	*salt and pepper*

Put the potatoes, beef, onion, tomatoes with the juice from the can, parsley and seasoning into a bowl and mix well. Turn into a casserole, cover and cook in a warm oven, 170°C, 325°F, Gas Mark 3 for 1 hour. Remove the lid and bake uncovered for a further 30 minutes. **Serves 4**

Bobotie

METRIC/IMPERIAL	AMERICAN
1 tablespoon oil	*1 tablespoon oil*
200 g./8 oz. button onions	*8 oz. button onions*
400 g./1 lb. minced beef	*1 lb. ground beef*
1 tablespoon flour	*1 tablespoon flour*
100 ml./scant ¼ pint water	*½ cup water*
1 beef stock cube, crumbled	*1 beef stock cube, crumbled*
2 tablespoons soy sauce	*2 tablespoons soy sauce*
1 teaspoon curry powder	*1 teaspoon curry powder*
½ teaspoon dried mixed herbs	*½ teaspoon dried mixed herbs*
salt and pepper	*salt and pepper*
2 eggs	*2 eggs*
250 ml./½ pint milk	*1¼ cups milk*
3 to 4 small bay leaves	*3 to 4 small bay leaves*
For the rice:	For the rice:
300 g./12 oz. long grain rice	*2 cups long grain rice*
750 ml./1½ pints water	*3¾ cups water*
½ teaspoon salt	*½ teaspoon salt*
pinch of powdered saffron	*pinch of powdered saffron*
100 g./4 oz. seedless raisins	*⅔ cup seedless raisins*

Heat the oil in a pan and fry the onions for about 5 minutes. Add the beef and fry for a further 5 minutes, stirring once or twice. Add the flour and cook for 2 minutes, then gradually stir in the water. Bring to the boil, stirring, then add the stock cube, soy sauce, curry powder, mixed herbs and seasoning. Turn into a casserole, cover and cook in a warm oven, 170°C, 325°F, Gas Mark 3 for 45 minutes.

Beat the eggs with the milk, pour over the meat and add the bay leaves. Cook uncovered for a further 30 minutes or until the top is pale golden.

For the rice, put the rice, water, salt and saffron into a casserole. Cover and cook in the oven with the meat for 1¼ hours, adding the raisins 10 minutes before the end of the cooking time. Serve the rice with the meat mixture.

Serves 4

Veal Chasseur ►

METRIC/IMPERIAL	AMERICAN
600 g./1½ lb. stewing veal	*1½ lb. stewing veal*
25 g./1 oz. butter	*2 tablespoons butter*
1 tablespoon oil	*1 tablespoon oil*
4 shallots, chopped	*4 shallots, chopped*
1 garlic clove, crushed	*1 garlic clove, crushed*
4 tomatoes, peeled, seeded and quartered	*4 tomatoes, peeled, seeded and quartered*
25 g./1 oz. flour	*¼ cup flour*
125 ml./¼ pint white wine	*⅝ cup white wine*
250 ml./½ pint stock	*1¼ cups stock*
salt and pepper	*salt and pepper*
150 g./6 oz. button mushrooms	*6 oz. button mushrooms*
10 black olives	*10 black olives*

Cut the meat into 2½ cm./1 in. cubes. Heat the butter and oil in a flameproof casserole and fry the shallots, garlic and meat together for about 10 minutes. Add the tomatoes to the casserole and cook for a further 5 minutes. Stir in the flour and cook for 2 minutes, then stir in the wine and stock. Bring to the boil, stirring all the time. Season with salt and pepper. Cover the casserole and cook in a moderate oven, 180°C, 350°F, Gas Mark 4 for 45 minutes. Add the mushrooms and olives and continue cooking for 15 minutes. **Serves 4**

Blanquette of Veal

METRIC/IMPERIAL	AMERICAN
600 g./1½ lb. stewing veal	*1½ lb. stewing veal*
50 g./2 oz. butter	*¼ cup butter*
10 small onions or shallots	*10 small onions or shallots*
50 g./2 oz. flour	*½ cup flour*
¾ l./1½ pints veal or chicken stock	*3¾ cups veal or chicken stock*
1 bouquet garni	*1 bouquet garni*
6 white peppercorns	*6 white peppercorns*
100 g./4 oz. button mushrooms	*4 oz. button mushrooms*
1 tablespoon lemon juice	*1 tablespoon lemon juice*
125 ml./¼ pint single cream	*⅝ cup light cream*
salt	*salt*

Trim the meat and cut into 5 cm./2 in. cubes. Melt the butter in a pan, add the meat and fry gently until it changes colour, but do not allow it to brown. Remove the meat from the pan with a slotted spoon and place in a casserole. Add the onions or shallots to the pan and fry these for 5 minutes without browning. Remove from the pan and add to the meat in the casserole.

Stir the flour into the butter remaining in the pan and cook for 2 minutes, stirring. Gradually stir in the stock and bring to the boil, stirring all the time. Add the bouquet garni, peppercorns and the ends of the stalks from the mushrooms. Cover and simmer gently for 20 minutes, then strain over the meat in the casserole. Add the mushrooms. Cover and cook in a moderate oven, 180°C, 350°F, Gas Mark 4 for 1½ hours. Stir in the lemon juice and cream and taste and adjust the seasoning before serving.

If wished, a border of mashed potato can be piped round the edge of the dish, as in the photograph, and quickly browned under the grill (broiler) before serving. **Serves 4**

Note: *If wishing to deep freeze this dish, do not add the lemon juice and cream before freezing. Reheat and stir in the lemon juice and cream just before use.*

Swiss Veal

A very good dish to serve for a dinner party, Swiss Veal improves with cooling and re-heating.

METRIC/IMPERIAL

400 to 600 g./1 to 1½ lb. boned leg of veal
40 g./1½ oz. flour
salt and freshly ground black pepper
75 g./3 oz. butter
1 onion, finely chopped
125 ml./¼ pint dry white wine
150 g./6 oz. button mushrooms, sliced
125 ml./¼ pint single cream
1 tablespoon chopped parsley
¼ teaspoon paprika

AMERICAN

1 to 1½ lb. boned leg of veal
6 tablespoons flour
salt and freshly ground black pepper
⅜ cup butter
1 onion, finely chopped
⅝ cup dry white wine
6 oz. button mushrooms, sliced
⅝ cup light cream
1 tablespoon chopped parsley
¼ teaspoon paprika

Cut the veal into narrow strips 5 cm./2 in. long and ¾ cm./¼ in. thick. Coat with the flour, seasoned with salt and pepper. Melt two-thirds of the butter in a frying pan and fry the veal and onion until lightly browned, stirring occasionally. Add the wine and cook over a moderate heat, stirring to a smooth consistency.

While the veal is cooking, fry the mushrooms in the remaining butter for 5 minutes. Remove from the heat and stir in the cream, parsley and paprika. In a casserole, combine the veal with the mushroom and cream mixture. Cover and cook in a cool oven, 150°C, 300°F, Gas Mark 2 for 45 minutes. If wished, sprinkle with more chopped parsley before serving with sauté potatoes and a green salad. **Serves 4 to 6**

Note: *Do not deep freeze this dish.*

Curried Meat Balls in Creamy Sauce

METRIC/IMPERIAL
25 g./1 oz. butter
2 medium-sized onions, finely chopped or grated
400 g./1 lb. lean minced veal or pork
½ teaspoon ground ginger
1 to 2 teaspoons curry powder
salt and pepper
50 g./2 oz. fresh white breadcrumbs
2 egg yolks
125 ml./¼ pint double cream

For the sauce:
50 g./2 oz. butter
25 g./1 oz. flour
1 to 2 teaspoons curry powder
375 ml./¾ pint stock
salt and pepper
1 tablespoon mango chutney

AMERICAN
2 tablespoons butter
2 medium-sized onions, finely chopped or grated
1 lb. lean ground veal or pork
½ teaspoon ground ginger
1 to 2 teaspoons curry powder
salt and pepper
1 cup fresh white breadcrumbs
2 egg yolks
⅝ cup heavy cream

For the sauce:
¼ cup butter
¼ cup flour
1 to 2 teaspoons curry powder
2 cups stock
salt and pepper
1 tablespoon mango chutney

Melt the butter in a small pan and cook the onions for 5 minutes. Turn into a bowl and add the veal or pork, ginger, curry powder, seasoning and breadcrumbs. Mix together and bind with the egg yolks and sufficient cream, about 3 to 4 tablespoons, to give a soft, creamy texture. Put into the refrigerator for 30 minutes to stiffen slightly, then form into balls the size of a walnut.

Melt the butter for the sauce in a large frying pan and fry the meat balls on all sides until golden brown. Remove from the pan and place in a casserole. Blend the flour and curry powder into the fat remaining in the pan and cook for 2 minutes. Gradually stir in the stock and bring to the boil, stirring all the time. Add the salt, pepper and chutney and pour into the casserole. Cover and cook in a moderate oven, 180°C, 350°F, Gas Mark 4 for 1 hour. Remove the casserole from the oven, allow to cool slightly, then stir in the remaining cream. Serve with boiled rice.

Serves 4

Note: *If wishing to deep freeze this dish, do not add the remaining cream before freezing. Reheat and stir in the cream just before serving.*

Osso Bucco ►

METRIC/IMPERIAL	AMERICAN
1¼ to 1¾ kg./3 to 4 lb. shin of veal	*3 to 4 lb. foreshank of veal*
flour	*flour*
6 tablespoons olive oil	*6 tablespoons olive oil*
1 medium-sized onion, thinly sliced	*1 medium-sized onion, thinly sliced*
1 medium-sized carrot, grated	*1 medium-sized carrot, grated*
1 celery stalk, chopped	*1 celery stalk, chopped*
8 tomatoes, peeled and chopped	*8 tomatoes, peeled and chopped*
1 tablespoon tomato purée	*1 tablespoon tomato purée*
50 g./2 oz. black olives	*¼ cup black olives*
125 ml./¼ pint white wine	*⅝ cup white wine*
125 ml./¼ pint stock	*⅝ cup stock*
salt and pepper	*salt and pepper*
4 tablespoons finely chopped parsley	*4 tablespoons finely chopped parsley*
1 to 2 garlic cloves, crushed	*1 to 2 garlic cloves, crushed*
finely grated rind of 1 small lemon	*finely grated rind of 1 small lemon*

Ask your butcher to cut the veal into 7½ cm./3 in. pieces. Coat the pieces in flour. Heat the oil in a large shallow pan, add the veal pieces a few at a time and fry until well browned. Remove from the pan and place in a casserole. Add the onion, carrot and celery to the oil remaining in the pan and fry gently for 5 to 10 minutes. Stir in the tomatoes, tomato purée, olives, wine, stock and seasoning. Bring to the boil and pour over the veal. Cover and cook in a warm oven, 170°C, 325°F, Gas Mark 3 for 2½ hours. Taste and adjust the seasoning.

Mix together the parsley, garlic and lemon rind and sprinkle over the top of the veal before serving. **Serves 6**

Czechoslovakian Casserole with Breadcrumb Dumplings

METRIC/IMPERIAL	AMERICAN
1 tablespoon oil	*1 tablespoon oil*
25 g./1 oz. butter	*2 tablespoons butter*
4 carrots, sliced	*4 carrots, sliced*
4 celery stalks, chopped	*4 celery stalks, chopped*
2 large onions, quartered	*2 large onions, quartered*
600 g./1½ lb. stewing veal	*1½ lb. stewing veal*
25 g./1 oz. flour	*¼ cup flour*
salt and pepper	*salt and pepper*
375 ml./¾ pint stock	*2 cups stock*
¼ teaspoon ground mace	*¼ teaspoon ground mace*
2 tablespoons chopped parsley	*2 tablespoons chopped parsley*
grated rind and juice of ½ lemon	*grated rind and juice of ½ lemon*
For the dumplings:	For the dumplings:
200 g./8 oz. fresh white breadcrumbs	*4 cups fresh white breadcrumbs*
4 tablespoons milk	*4 tablespoons milk*
50 g./2 oz. butter or margarine	*¼ cup butter or margarine*
1 egg, beaten	*1 egg, beaten*
½ teaspoon salt	*½ teaspoon salt*
pinch of pepper	*pinch of pepper*

Melt the oil and butter in a large flameproof casserole. Add the carrots, celery and onions, cover and cook gently for 10 minutes. Cut the veal into 2½ cm./1 in. cubes and coat with the flour, seasoned with salt and pepper. Add to the vegetables and cook for a further 5 to 10 minutes, stirring frequently. Gradually stir in the stock and bring to the boil, stirring all the time. Add the mace and half the parsley. Cover and cook in a moderate oven, 180°C, 350°F, Gas Mark 4 for 1 hour.

For the dumplings, soak the breadcrumbs in the milk. Melt the butter or margarine in a saucepan, but do not allow it to become too hot. Beat in the egg, the soaked breadcrumbs and seasoning. Beat well together. Shape into eight small balls. Cook the dumplings in boiling salted water for 5 minutes. Drain and add to the casserole 10 minutes before the end of cooking time.

Just before serving, gently stir the lemon juice into the casserole and serve sprinkled with the lemon rind and remaining parsley. **Serves 4 to 6**

Lamb Curry with Apricots

METRIC/IMPERIAL	AMERICAN
200 g./8 oz. dried apricots	*$1^1/_3$ cups dried apricots*
500 ml./1 pint water	*$2^1/_2$ cups water*
50 g./2 oz. butter	*$^1/_4$ cup butter*
4 onions, chopped	*4 onions, chopped*
800 g./2 lb. boneless lean lamb, from the shoulder, fillet or leg, cut into cubes	*2 lb. boneless lean lamb, from the shoulder, fillet or leg, cut into cubes*
2 teaspoons ground coriander	*2 teaspoons ground coriander*
2 teaspoons ground cumin	*2 teaspoons ground cumin*
1 teaspoon ground cinnamon	*1 teaspoon ground cinnamon*
salt and pepper	*salt and pepper*

Put the apricots into a bowl, cover with the water and leave to soak overnight.

Melt the butter in a flameproof casserole and fry the onions for about 5 minutes or until soft and golden. Add the lamb, increase the heat and cook until browned on all sides. Add the spices and seasoning and cook, stirring, for a further 2 to 3 minutes. Add the apricots and the water in which they were soaked. Cover and cook in a warm oven, 170°C, 325°F, Gas Mark 3 for 2 hours. Taste and adjust the seasoning before serving.

Serves 6 to 8

Turkish Lamb

METRIC/IMPERIAL
3 lamb fillets
50 g./2 oz. flour
4 tablespoons olive oil
2 onions, chopped
2 garlic cloves, crushed
2 green peppers, seeded and chopped
750 ml./1½ pints tomato juice
2 teaspoons cumin seeds
2 teaspoons black peppercorns
juice of 1 lemon
salt

To garnish:
1 mint sprig
2 to 4 lemon wedges

AMERICAN
about 2 lb. boned leg of lamb
½ cup flour
4 tablespoons olive oil
2 onions, chopped
2 garlic cloves, crushed
2 green peppers, seeded and chopped
3¾ cups tomato juice
2 teaspoons cumin seeds
2 teaspoons black peppercorns
juice of 1 lemon
salt

To garnish:
1 mint sprig
2 to 4 lemon wedges

Cut each lamb fillet in half or the leg of lamb into six thick pieces and coat with the flour. Heat the oil in a large pan and fry the meat quickly on all sides until golden brown. Remove from the pan and place in a casserole. Add the onions, garlic and peppers to the pan and cook for a further 5 minutes. Gradually stir in the tomato juice and bring to the boil. Stir in the cumin seeds, peppercorns and lemon juice and season with salt. Pour over the meat in the casserole and stir lightly. Cover and cook in a cool oven, 150°C, 300°F, Gas Mark 2 for 3 hours.

Taste and adjust the seasoning before serving. Garnish with mint and lemon wedges.

Serves 4

Note: *This unusual casserole is best served with boiled rice and a Turkish cucumber salad. To make this, peel and chop a cucumber, put into a colander and sprinkle with a teaspoon of salt. Leave to drain for 30 minutes, then mix with 125 ml./¼ pint (⅝ cup) yogurt, a teaspoon of cumin seed, a tablespoon of wine vinegar, a crushed clove of garlic and a tablespoon of chopped mint.*

French Lamb Casserole

METRIC/IMPERIAL
400 g./1 lb. button onions
2 garlic cloves, crushed
25 g./1 oz. dripping
600 g./1½ lb. stewing lamb, cut into cubes
40 g./1½ oz. flour
500 ml./1 pint stock, or water and 1 stock cube
salt and pepper
70 g./2¼ oz. can tomato purée
1 bouquet garni
150 g./6 oz. fresh shelled or frozen peas
1 teaspoon chopped parsley

AMERICAN
1 lb. button onions
2 garlic cloves, crushed
2 tablespoons dripping
1½ lb. stewing lamb, cut into cubes
6 tablespoons flour
2½ cups stock, or water and 1 stock cube
salt and pepper
2¼ oz. can tomato purée
1 bouquet garni
6 oz. fresh shelled or frozen peas
1 teaspoon chopped parsley

Fry the onions and garlic in the dripping in a pan or flameproof casserole until pale golden. Add the meat and cook until browned on all sides. Sprinkle over the flour and cook over a gentle heat for about 5 minutes or until the flour is golden. Gradually stir in the stock or water and stock cube and bring to the boil, stirring all the time. Add the seasoning, tomato purée and bouquet garni. If cooking in a pan, transfer to a casserole. Cover and cook in a warm oven, 170°C, 325°F, Gas Mark 3 for 1¼ hours.

Stir in the peas and cook for a further 20 minutes. Remove the bouquet garni. Taste and adjust the seasoning. Serve sprinkled with parsley.

Serves 4

Lamb and Bean Hotpot

METRIC/IMPERIAL
300 g./12 oz. haricot beans, soaked overnight and drained
salt and pepper
2 tablespoons oil
2 large onions, sliced
4 streaky bacon rashers, chopped
600 g./1½ lb. stewing lamb, chopped
125 g./5 oz. can tomato purée
2 large carrots, sliced
2 parsnips, sliced
2 celery stalks, chopped
1 parsley sprig
1 teaspoon chopped fresh thyme
1 bay leaf

AMERICAN
2 cups haricot (dried white) beans, soaked overnight and drained
salt and pepper
2 tablespoons oil
2 large onions, sliced
4 fatty bacon slices, chopped
1½ lb. stewing lamb, chopped
5 oz. can tomato purée
2 large carrots, sliced
2 parsnips, sliced
2 celery stalks, chopped
1 parsley sprig
1 teaspoon chopped fresh thyme
1 bay leaf

Put the beans into a pan with fresh cold water to cover and a little salt and bring to the boil. Cover and simmer gently for 1 hour. Drain and reserve the liquid.

Heat the oil in a frying pan and fry the onions and bacon gently for 5 minutes. Add the lamb and cook for a further 5 minutes or until browned on all sides. Turn into a casserole with the drained beans, tomato purée, carrots, parsnips, celery, herbs and seasoning. Pour over 500 ml./1 pint (2½ cups) of the reserved bean liquid and mix well. Cover and cook in a warm oven, 170°C, 325°F, Gas Mark 3 for 2 hours. Remove the bay leaf and parsley sprig. Taste and adjust the seasoning before serving, garnished with parsley. **Serves 4 to 6**

◄

Spring Lamb Casserole

METRIC/IMPERIAL	AMERICAN
800 g./2 lb. scrag end of lamb, cut into cutlets	*2 lb. neck slices of lamb*
500 g./1 pint stock or water	*2½ cups stock or water*
6 new carrots, sliced	*6 new carrots, sliced*
1 small swede, diced	*1 small rutabaga, diced*
2 small turnips, diced	*2 small turnips, diced*
2 leeks, sliced	*2 leeks, sliced*
1 onion, chopped	*1 onion, chopped*
6 new potatoes, diced	*6 new potatoes, diced*
salt and pepper	*salt and pepper*
100 g./4 oz. fresh shelled or frozen peas	*4 oz. fresh shelled or frozen peas*
1 tablespoon chopped parsley	*1 tablespoon chopped parsley*

Trim the excess fat off the cutlets (slices) and put them into a casserole with the stock or water, carrots, swede (rutabaga), turnips, leeks, onion and potatoes. Season well with salt and pepper. Cover and cook in a moderate oven, 180°C, 350°F, Gas Mark 4 for 1¾ hours. Stir in the peas and cook for a further 15 minutes. Taste and adjust the seasoning and sprinkle with chopped parsley before serving. **Serves 4 to 6**

Lamb Layer Casserole

This is a good way of using up leftover roast lamb together with the gravy and is a useful 'complete-meal-in-one-pot' dish.

METRIC/IMPERIAL	AMERICAN
25 g./1 oz. butter	*2 tablespoons butter*
1 large onion, chopped	*1 large onion, chopped*
400 g./1 lb. cooked lamb, cubed	*1 lb. cooked lamb, cubed*
125 ml./¼ pint thick, rich gravy	*⅝ cup thick, rich gravy*
1 small cabbage, separated into leaves	*1 small cabbage, separated into leaves*
salt and pepper	*salt and pepper*
200 g./8 oz. long grain rice	*1⅓ cups long grain rice*
2 carrots, thinly sliced	*2 carrots, thinly sliced*
1 small turnip, thinly sliced	*1 small turnip, thinly sliced*
250 ml./½ pint stock	*1¼ cups stock*

Melt the butter in a pan and fry the onion gently for 5 minutes. Stir in the lamb and gravy and cook gently for 2 to 3 minutes. Transfer to a large casserole. Place the cabbage on top of the meat. Season with salt and a little pepper. Cover with the rice and then with a layer of carrots and turnip. Season with salt and pepper. Pour the stock gently over the top. Cover tightly and cook in a moderately hot oven, 200°C, 400°F, Gas Mark 6 for 1 hour. **Serves 4 to 6**

Lamb, Chick Pea and Bean Casserole

METRIC/IMPERIAL
1¼ kg./3 lb. stewing lamb
150 g./6 oz. dried chick peas, soaked overnight and drained
150 g./6 oz. soya beans, soaked overnight and drained
4 onions
1 l./2 pints water
salt and freshly ground black pepper
425 g./15 oz. can tomatoes
juice of 1 large lemon
1 teaspoon ground turmeric

AMERICAN
3 lb. stewing lamb
1 cup dried chick peas (garbanzos), soaked overnight and drained
1 cup soya beans, soaked overnight and drained
4 onions
5 cups water
salt and freshly ground black pepper
15 oz. can tomatoes
juice of 1 large lemon
1 teaspoon ground turmeric

Put the lamb into a large casserole with the chick peas and soya beans. Quarter three of the onions and add to the casserole with the water and seasoning. Cover and cook in a cool oven, 150°C, 300°F, Gas Mark 2 for 1½ hours.

Add the tomatoes, lemon juice and turmeric, re-cover and cook for a further 1½ hours. Skim off any excess fat and taste and adjust the seasoning. Just before serving, finely chop the remaining onion and add to the casserole. **Serves 6**

Traditional Lancashire Hotpot

METRIC/IMPERIAL
600 g./ 1½ lb. middle or best end of neck lamb cutlets
1 tablespoon flour
salt and pepper
2 lamb's kidneys
4 medium-sized onions, sliced
200 g./8 oz. carrots, diced
600 g./ 1½ lb. potatoes, sliced
375 ml./¾ pint stock

AMERICAN
1½ lb. lamb rib chops
1 tablespoon flour
salt and pepper
2 lamb's kidneys
4 medium-sized onions, sliced
8 oz. carrots, diced
1½ lb. potatoes, sliced
2 cups stock

Trim off any excess fat from the lamb cutlets (chops) and coat with the flour, seasoned with salt and pepper. Remove the skin and core from the kidneys and cut them into slices. Place layers of meat, onions, kidneys, carrots and potatoes in a large casserole, seasoning each layer lightly with salt and pepper, and finishing with a layer of potatoes. Pour over the stock, cover and cook in a moderate oven, 180°C, 350°F, Gas Mark 4 for 2 hours. Remove the lid of the casserole and cook for a further 30 minutes to brown the potatoes. **Serves 4**

Moussaka I

METRIC/IMPERIAL	AMERICAN
4 large aubergines, sliced	*4 large eggplants, sliced*
salt and pepper	*salt and pepper*
oil for frying	*oil for frying*
600 g./ 1½ lb. shoulder of lamb, coarsely minced	*1½ lb. shoulder of lamb, coarsely ground*
600 g./ 1½ lb. onions, chopped	*1½ lb. onions, chopped*
1 garlic clove, crushed	*1 garlic clove, crushed*
65 g./ 2½ oz. flour	*⅝ cup flour*
425 g./ 15 oz. can tomatoes	*15 oz. can tomatoes*
¼ teaspoon dried mixed herbs	*¼ teaspoon dried mixed herbs*
2 tablespoons chopped parsley	*2 tablespoons chopped parsley*
40 g./ 1½ oz. butter	*3 tablespoons butter*
375 ml./¾ pint milk	*2 cups milk*
150 g./ 6 oz. strong Cheddar cheese, grated	*1½ cups grated strong Cheddar cheese*

Sprinkle the aubergines (eggplants) with salt and leave for 30 minutes, then drain off the liquid. Heat a little oil in a frying pan and fry the aubergines (eggplants) a few at a time for 2 to 3 minutes on each side. Remove from the pan and put on one side. Aubergines (eggplants) tend to absorb a great deal of oil when fried, but do not use too much or the dish will be greasy.

Heat another tablespoon of oil in the pan and fry the meat for about 5 minutes. Add the onions and garlic and cook for a further 10 minutes. Blend in 25 g./1 oz. (2 tablespoons) of the flour, the juice from the can of tomatoes, the herbs and seasoning and bring to the boil, stirring.

Lightly grease a casserole and arrange layers of aubergine (eggplant) slices, then meat mixture and then tomatoes in it, finishing with a circular pattern of aubergine (eggplant) slices.

Melt the butter in a pan, add the remaining flour and cook for 1 minute. Gradually stir in the milk and bring to the boil, stirring all the time. Remove from the heat and stir in the cheese and seasoning. When the cheese has melted, pour the sauce over the aubergines (eggplants). Cook the moussaka, uncovered, in a moderately hot oven, 190°C, 375°F, Gas Mark 5 for 45 minutes. **Serves 6**

Casseroled Lambs' Hearts

METRIC/IMPERIAL	AMERICAN
4 small lambs' hearts	*4 small lambs' hearts*
15 g./½ oz. butter	*1 tablespoon butter*
2 medium-sized onions, finely chopped	*2 medium-sized onions, finely chopped*
1 small cooking apple, peeled and grated	*1 small cooking apple, peeled and grated*
25 g./ 1 oz. fresh white breadcrumbs	*½ cup fresh white breadcrumbs*
¼ teaspoon dried mixed herbs	*¼ teaspoon dried mixed herbs*
salt and pepper	*salt and pepper*
1 tablespoon flour	*1 tablespoon flour*
25 g./ 1 oz. dripping	*2 tablespoons dripping*
2 carrots, sliced	*2 carrots, sliced*
2 small turnips, chopped	*2 small turnips, chopped*
250 ml./½ pint stock	*1¼ cups stock*

Wash the hearts, slit them open and remove any tubers, then wash again. Melt the butter in a frying pan and fry half of one of the onions over a gentle heat for 5 minutes. Add the apple and cook for 5 minutes longer. Stir in the breadcrumbs, herbs and seasoning. Fill the hearts with this stuffing, then tie them into their original shape with string. Coat with the flour, seasoned with salt and pepper.

Melt the dripping in a flameproof casserole and fry the hearts until browned. Remove from the pan and put on one side. Add the remaining onions, the carrots and turnips and cook gently for 10 minutes. Replace the hearts in the casserole, pour over the stock and cover. Cook in a warm oven, 170°C, 325°F, Gas Mark 3 for 2 hours. Taste and adjust the seasoning before serving. **Serves 4**

Moussaka II

This version of Moussaka uses beef instead of lamb and has a much richer topping.

METRIC/IMPERIAL
400 g./1 lb. aubergines, thinly sliced
salt and pepper
oil for frying
2 large onions, thinly sliced
1 garlic clove, crushed
400 g./1 lb. lean beef, minced
425 g./15 oz. can tomatoes
2 tablespoons tomato purée
2 eggs
125 ml./¼ pint single cream
50 g./2 oz. grated Cheddar cheese
25 g./1 oz. grated Parmesan cheese

AMERICAN
1 lb. eggplants, thinly sliced
salt and pepper
oil for frying
2 large onions, thinly sliced
1 garlic clove, crushed
1 lb. lean beef, ground
15 oz. can tomatoes
2 tablespoons tomato purée
2 eggs
⅝ cup light cream
½ cup grated Cheddar cheese
¼ cup grated Parmesan cheese

Sprinkle the aubergines (eggplants) with salt and leave for 30 minutes, then drain off the liquid. Heat a little oil in a frying pan and fry the aubergines (eggplants), a few at a time, for 2 to 3 minutes on each side. Remove from the pan and put on one side. Aubergines (eggplants) tend to absorb a great deal of oil when fried, but do not use too much or the dish will be greasy.

Fry the onions and garlic in 1 tablespoon oil until pale golden. Add the beef and cook for about 10 minutes, stirring occasionally. Add the tomatoes, with the juice from the can, and tomato purée and mix well. Bring to the boil and simmer for 20 to 25 minutes. Season with salt and pepper. Arrange alternate layers of aubergines (eggplants) and the beef mixture in a casserole. Cover and bake in a moderate oven, 180°C, 350°F, Gas Mark 4 for 40 minutes. Beat the eggs and cream together and stir in the cheese. Pour on to the casserole mixture and bake uncovered for a further 15 to 20 minutes or until the topping is firm, well risen and golden brown.

Serves 4

Irish Casserole with Parsley Dumplings

METRIC/IMPERIAL
1¼ kg./3 lb. middle neck or scrag end of lamb, cut into pieces
25 g./1 oz. flour
salt and pepper
3 large onions, chopped
400 g./1 lb. potatoes, sliced
1 tablespoon pearl barley
½ teaspoon dried mixed herbs
750 ml./1½ pints boiling water or stock

For the dumplings:
100 g./4 oz. self-raising flour
pinch of salt
pinch of pepper
50 g./2 oz. shredded suet
2 tablespoons chopped parsley
4 tablespoons cold water

AMERICAN
3 lb. middle neck or scrag end of lamb, cut into pieces
¼ cup flour
salt and pepper
3 large onions, chopped
1 lb. potatoes, sliced
1 tablespoon pearl barley
½ teaspoon dried mixed herbs
3¾ cups boiling water or stock

For the dumplings:
1 cup self-rising flour
pinch of salt
pinch of pepper
¼ cup shredded suet
2 tablespoons chopped parsley
4 tablespoons cold water

Coat the pieces of lamb with the flour, seasoned with salt and pepper. Put into a large casserole with the onions, potatoes, barley and herbs. Pour over the boiling water or stock. Put into a warm oven, 170°C, 325°F, Gas Mark 3 and cook for 2½ hours.

For the dumplings, sift the flour, salt and pepper into a mixing bowl. Add the suet and parsley and bind with the water to give a soft dough. Divide the mixture into eight portions and roll into small balls with lightly floured hands. Skim off any scum from the surface of the casserole mixture, add the dumplings and cook for a further 30 minutes.

Serves 4

Lamb Julienne ►

METRIC/IMPERIAL	AMERICAN
1 to 1¼ kg./2½ to 3 lb. shoulder of lamb	*2½ to 3 lb. shoulder of lamb*
1 l/2 pints water	*5 cups water*
1 bay leaf	*1 bay leaf*
1 medium-sized onion, chopped	*1 medium-sized onion, chopped*
salt and freshly ground black pepper	*salt and freshly ground black pepper*
3 tablespoons flour	*3 tablespoons flour*
1 teaspoon curry powder	*1 teaspoon curry powder*
8 small onions	*8 small onions*
8 carrots, cut into sticks	*8 carrots, cut into sticks*
For the dumplings:	For the dumplings:
40 g./1½ oz. butter	*3 tablespoons butter*
50 g./2 oz. fresh white breadcrumbs	*1 cup fresh white breadcrumbs*
150 g./6 oz. self-raising flour	*1½ cups self-rising flour*
½ teaspoon salt	*½ teaspoon salt*
1 teaspoon dehydrated onion	*1 teaspoon onion flakes*
2 tablespoons oil	*2 tablespoons oil*
little milk	*little milk*

Bone the lamb and cut the meat into cubes, putting the fat on one side. Put the bones into a saucepan with the water, bay leaf, onion and salt and pepper. Bring slowly to the boil, remove any scum, then cover and simmer gently for 2 hours. Strain and reserve the stock.

Put the lamb fat into a frying pan, place over a gentle heat and fry gently until all the fat runs out. Strain and reserve.

Sift together the flour, curry powder, salt and pepper, then coat the lamb cubes with this mixture. Heat 25 g./1 oz. (2 tablespoons) of the fat in a frying pan and fry the meat in the fat until well browned. Stir in any excess flour. Gradually add 750 ml./1½ pints (3¾ cups) of the lamb stock and bring to the boil, stirring all the time. Transfer to a casserole and add the onions and carrots. Cover and cook in a warm oven, 170°C, 325°F, Gas Mark 3 for 1 hour.

For the dumplings: melt the butter in a pan, stir in the breadcrumbs and cook gently, stirring frequently, until golden. Sift together the flour and salt, then add the dehydrated onion. Stir in the oil and enough milk to give a soft, but manageable dough. Shape into balls, coat with the fried breadcrumbs and arrange in the casserole. Cover and cook for a further 1 hour.

Serves 6

Savoury Breasts of Lamb

METRIC/IMPERIAL	AMERICAN
2 × 600 g./1½ lb. breasts of lamb	*2 × 1½ lb. breasts of lamb*
750 ml./1½ pints water	*3¾ cups water*
1 onion, chopped	*1 onion, chopped*
1 carrot, chopped	*1 carrot, chopped*
1 small turnip, chopped	*1 small turnip, chopped*
few parsley stalks	*few parsley stalks*
salt and pepper	*salt and pepper*
15 g./½ oz. dripping	*1 tablespoon dripping*
25 g./1 oz. flour	*¼ cup flour*
2 tablespoons chopped parsley	*2 tablespoons chopped parsley*
For the stuffing:	For the stuffing:
50 g./2 oz. crustless white bread	*2 oz. crustless white bread*
25 g./1 oz. butter	*2 tablespoons butter*
1 onion, very finely chopped	*1 onion, very finely chopped*
2 lamb's kidneys	*2 lamb's kidneys*
50 g./2 oz. cooked ham, finely chopped	*2 oz. cooked ham, finely chopped*
100 g./4 oz. cooked spinach finely chopped	*4 oz. cooked spinach, finely chopped*
salt and pepper	*salt and pepper*
1 teaspoon chopped fresh rosemary	*1 teaspoon chopped fresh rosemary*

Ask the butcher to bone the lamb for you, or do this yourself. Put the lamb bones into a large saucepan with the water, onion, carrot, turnip, parsley stalks and seasoning. Bring slowly to the boil, remove all the grey scum, cover and simmer gently for 1½ hours.

Soak the bread for the stuffing in cold water, then squeeze dry in your hands and put into a bowl. Melt the butter in a small pan and fry the onion gently for 5 minutes. Remove the skin and core from the kidneys and cut them into small pieces. Add to the pan and cook gently for 2 to 3 minutes. Turn into the bowl with the bread and mix in all the remaining stuffing ingredients.

Place the two breasts of lamb on a board and trim off all the excess fat. Spread the stuffing over half of each joint, then fold the other half over the top. Tie in two or three places with string to keep the stuffing in place. Melt the dripping in a large frying pan or saucepan, add the breasts of lamb and fry on both sides until they are golden. Transfer to a casserole. Lower the heat and stir the flour into the fat in the frying pan. Cook very gently, stirring frequently, until the flour is golden brown, then gradually stir in the strained stock from cooking the bones. Bring the sauce to the boil, stirring all the time. Taste and adjust the seasoning, then pour over the lamb in the casserole. Cover and cook in a warm oven, 170°C, 325°F, Gas Mark 3 for 2 hours. Take the lamb out of the casserole, remove the string and arrange on a heated serving dish. Remove any excess fat from the sauce, taste and adjust the seasoning, then strain over the lamb and sprinkle with parsley.

Serves 4

◄

Lamb in Yogurt Sauce

METRIC/IMPERIAL

600 g./1½ lb. boned leg or shoulder of lamb
25 g./1 oz. butter
1 tablespoon oil
1 large onion, chopped
25 g./1 oz. flour
250 ml./½ pint stock
salt and pepper
1 tablespoon capers
2 pickled dill cucumbers, sliced
grated rind of 1 lemon
1 tablespoon chopped parsley
250 ml./½ pint natural yogurt

AMERICAN

1½ lb. boned leg or shoulder of lamb
2 tablespoons butter
1 tablespoon oil
1 large onion, chopped
¼ cup flour
1¼ cups stock
salt and pepper
1 tablespoon capers
2 pickled dill cucumbers, sliced
grated rind of 1 lemon
1 tablespoon chopped parsley
1¼ cups natural yogurt

Cut the lamb into 2½ cm./1 in. cubes. Heat the butter and oil in a flameproof casserole and fry the onion gently for 5 minutes. Add the lamb to the casserole and fry for 3 minutes, stirring occasionally. Add the flour and cook for 1 minute. Add the stock and bring to the boil, stirring all the time. Season with salt and pepper and add the capers, dill cucumbers, lemon rind and parsley. Cover the casserole and cook in a warm oven, 170°C, 325°F, Gas Mark 3 for 1½ hours. Take the casserole out of the oven, allow it to cool slightly, then stir in the yogurt. Put over a very gentle heat to heat the yogurt, but do not allow the sauce to boil. Taste and adjust the seasoning before serving. **Serves 4**

Note: *If wishing to deep freeze this dish, do not add the yogurt before freezing. Reheat and stir in the yogurt just before serving.*

Lambs' Tongues with Barbecue Sauce

METRIC/IMPERIAL

600 g./1½ lb. lambs' tongues
1 onion, chopped
1 bouquet garni
salt and pepper
156 g./5½ oz. can condensed cream of tomato soup
1 tablespoon Worcestershire sauce
2 tablespoons made mustard
2 tablespoons raisins
1 dill pickle, finely chopped

AMERICAN

1½ lb. lambs' tongues
1 onion, chopped
1 bouquet garni
salt and pepper
5½ oz. can condensed cream of tomato soup
1 tablespoon Worcestershire sauce
2 tablespoons made mustard
2 tablespoons raisins
1 dill pickle, finely chopped

Put the lambs' tongues into a pan with cold water to cover, the onion, bouquet garni and seasoning. Bring slowly to the boil, remove any scum, then cover and simmer gently for 2 hours or until very tender. Drain and reserve the stock. When cool enough to handle, cut off the root end, remove any bones and skin the tongues. Place the tongues in a casserole.

Mix the soup with 125 ml./¼ pint (⅝ cup) of the reserved tongue stock, the Worcestershire sauce, mustard, raisins and dill pickle. Pour over the tongue in the casserole, cover and cook in a moderate oven, 180°C, 350°F, Gas Mark 4 for 1 hour. Taste and adjust the seasoning before serving. **Serves 4**

Curried Lamb

METRIC/IMPERIAL

25 g./1 oz. desiccated coconut
125 ml./¼ pint boiling water
25 g./1 oz. butter
600 g./1½ lb. lean lamb (fillet, shoulder or leg), cut into pieces
2 onions, chopped
2 garlic cloves, crushed
1 teaspoon powdered ginger
2 teaspoons coriander seeds
½ teaspoon ground turmeric
½ to 1 teaspoon chilli powder
1 teaspoon ground cumin
1½ teaspoons garam masala
70 g./2¼ oz. can tomato purée
salt

AMERICAN

2 tablespoons shredded coconut
⅝ cup boiling water
2 tablespoons butter
1½ lb. lean lamb (fillet, shoulder or leg), cut into pieces
2 onions, chopped
2 garlic cloves, crushed
1 teaspoon powdered ginger
2 teaspoons coriander seeds
½ teaspoon ground turmeric
½ to 1 teaspoon chilli powder
1 teaspoon ground cumin
1½ teaspoons garam masala
2¼ oz. can tomato purée
salt

Put the coconut into a jug, pour over the boiling water and leave for 10 minutes. Melt the butter in a large pan or flameproof casserole and gently fry the meat with the onions, garlic and all the spices for about 10 minutes, stirring well. Add the tomato purée to the meat mixture and stir in the strained coconut liquid. Season with salt. Either cover the flameproof casserole or transfer from the pan to a casserole and cover. Cook in a cool oven, 150°C, 300°F, Gas Mark 2 for 3 hours. Check the casserole two or three times during cooking and, if necessary, stir in a little more water. Skim off any excess fat before serving with boiled rice and poppadums. **Serves 4**

Pork Chops with Cabbage ►

METRIC/IMPERIAL	AMERICAN
600 g./1½ lb. cabbage (a Savoy or similar would be ideal), finely shredded	*1½ lb. cabbage (a Savoy or similar would be ideal), finely shredded*
salt and black pepper	*salt and black pepper*
25 g./1 oz. butter	*2 tablespoons butter*
1 large onion, finely chopped	*1 large onion, finely chopped*
1 garlic clove, crushed	*1 garlic clove, crushed*
4 pork chops	*4 pork chops*
250 ml./½ pint dry cider	*1¼ cups dry cider*
4 tablespoons double cream	*4 tablespoons heavy cream*
50 g./2 oz. Cheddar cheese, grated	*½ cup Cheddar cheese, grated*

Cook the cabbage in boiling salted water for 5 minutes. Drain and turn into a bowl. Melt half the butter in a frying pan, add the onion and garlic and fry gently for 10 minutes. Add to the cabbage, mix lightly and turn half the mixture into a casserole.

Melt the remaining butter in the frying pan. Season the chops with salt and pepper and fry quickly on both sides until golden brown. Remove from the pan and place on the cabbage mixture in the casserole. Cover with the remaining cabbage mixture. Pour the cider into the pan and boil over a moderate heat until the cider has reduced to about 4 tablespoons. Remove from the heat, stir in the cream and pour into the casserole. Cover and cook in a moderate oven, 180°C, 350°F, Gas Mark 4 for 45 minutes. Sprinkle the cheese on top and bake uncovered for a further 20 to 30 minutes or until the cheese is golden brown. **Serves 4**

Pork Chops with Plums

METRIC/IMPERIAL	AMERICAN
4 pork loin chops	*4 pork loin chops*
300 g./12 oz. plums, stoned	*12 oz. plums, pitted*
2 tablespoons sugar	*2 tablespoons sugar*
2 tablespoons water	*2 tablespoons water*
¼ teaspoon ground cinnamon	*¼ teaspoon ground cinnamon*
4 cloves	*4 cloves*
125 ml./¼ pint red wine	*⅝ cup red wine*
salt and pepper	*salt and pepper*

Put the pork chops into a frying pan without any fat over a low heat. As the fat runs out, increase the heat and cook on both sides until lightly browned. Remove from the pan and place in a casserole.

Put the plums into a saucepan with the sugar, water, cinnamon and cloves. Simmer gently for 15 minutes. Remove the cloves and either put through a sieve or blend in a liquidizer for 1 minute. Add the wine to the plum purée and season to taste with salt and pepper. Pour over the chops in the casserole. Cover and cook in a moderate oven, 180°C, 350°F, Gas Mark 4 for 1 hour. Taste and adjust the seasoning before serving. **Serves 4**

Summer Pork Casserole with Cream

METRIC/IMPERIAL
600 g./1½ lb. pork fillet
2 tablespoons oil
25 g./1 oz. butter
1 onion, chopped
1 tablespoon paprika
25 g./1 oz. flour
250 ml./½ pint stock
4 tablespoons sherry
1 tablespoon tomato purée
2 tomatoes, peeled, seeded and quartered
150 g./6 oz. button mushrooms
8 stuffed green olives, sliced
salt and pepper
125 ml./¼ pint double cream

AMERICAN
1½ lb. pork tenderloin
2 tablespoons oil
2 tablespoons butter
1 onion, chopped
1 tablespoon paprika
¼ cup flour
1¼ cups stock
4 tablespoons sherry
1 tablespoon tomato purée
2 tomatoes, peeled, seeded and quartered
6 oz. button mushrooms
8 stuffed green olives, sliced
salt and pepper
⅝ cup heavy cream

Cut the pork into 3¾ cm./1½ in. pieces. Heat the oil and butter in a pan and fry the meat on all sides for about 5 minutes. Remove from the pan with a slotted spoon and place in a casserole. Add the onion to the pan and fry for 5 minutes. Stir in the paprika and flour and cook for a further 2 minutes. Gradually stir in the stock and bring to the boil, stirring all the time until the mixture thickens. Add the sherry and tomato purée and pour into the casserole. Add the tomatoes to the casserole with the mushrooms. Cover and cook in a moderate oven, 180°C, 350°F, Gas Mark 4 for 1 hour.

Stir in the olives and taste and adjust the seasoning. Stir in most of the cream and spoon the remainder over the top before serving.

Serves 4

Note: *If wishing to deep freeze this dish, do not add the cream before freezing. Reheat and stir in the cream just before serving.*

Pork Chops with Cider

METRIC IMPERIAL	AMERICAN
25 g./1 oz. butter	*2 tablespoons butter*
1 tablespoon oil	*1 tablespoon oil*
4 pork chops	*4 pork chops*
100 g./4 oz. button onions	*4 oz. button onions*
200 g./8 oz. tomatoes, peeled and quartered	*8 oz. tomatoes, peeled and quartered*
2 celery stalks, cut in 2.5 cm./1 in. pieces	*2 celery stalks, cut in 1 in. pieces*
2 dessert apples, cored and sliced	*2 dessert apples, cored and sliced*
100 g./4 oz. button mushrooms	*4 oz. button mushrooms*
25 g./1 oz. flour	*1/4 cup flour*
375 ml./3/4 pint stock	*2 cups stock*
125 ml./1/4 pint dry cider	*5/8 cup dry cider*
1 tablespoon chopped fresh thyme	*1 tablespoon chopped fresh thyme*
salt and black pepper	*salt and black pepper*
1 tablespoon chopped parsley	*1 tablespoon chopped parsley*

Heat the butter and oil together in a large frying pan and fry the chops on both sides until browned. Remove from the pan and place in a casserole. Add the onions, tomatoes, celery, apples and mushrooms to the fat remaining in the pan and cook for 5 minutes. Sprinkle in the flour and cook for 2 minutes. Gradually stir in the stock and cider and bring to the boil, stirring all the time. Add the thyme and seasoning and pour over the chops in the casserole. Cover and cook in a moderate oven, 180°C, 350°F, Gas Mark 4 for 1 hour. Taste and adjust the seasoning before serving sprinkled with the chopped parsley.

Serves 4

Pork and Eggs ►

This is a Chinese recipe which I have adapted for cooking in a casserole.

METRIC/IMPERIAL	AMERICAN
1 tablespoon oil	*1 tablespoon oil*
600 g./1½ lb. lean pork, cut into large dice	*1½ lb. lean pork, cut into large dice*
375 ml./¾ pint water	*2 cups water*
2 tablespoons soy sauce	*2 tablespoons soy sauce*
2 tablespoons sherry	*2 tablespoons sherry*
salt	*salt*
4 eggs	*4 eggs*
1 bunch spring onions, chopped	*1 bunch scallions, chopped*

Heat the oil in a flameproof casserole and fry the pork on all sides until just golden. Add the water, soy sauce, sherry and salt. Cover the casserole and cook in a moderate oven, 180°C, 350°F, Gas Mark 4 for 1 hour. Boil the eggs for 8 minutes, then cool and remove the shells. Make a small slit in the side of each egg and add to the pork with the spring onions (scallions). Re-cover and cook for a further 10 minutes.

Serves 4

Note: *This dish cannot be deep frozen after the eggs have been added. If wishing to freeze, cook for 1 hour, freeze, then reheat with the eggs and spring onions (scallions).*

Spare Ribs of Pork with Spicy Orange and Cranberry Sauce

METRIC/IMPERIAL	AMERICAN
2 tablespoons oil	*2 tablespoons oil*
4 spare rib chops	*4 spare rib chops*
1 onion, chopped	*1 onion, chopped*
184 g./6½ oz. jar cranberry sauce	*6½ oz. jar cranberry sauce*
finely grated rind and juice of 1 orange	*finely grated rind and juice of 1 orange*
1 tablespoon Worcestershire sauce	*1 tablespoon Worcestershire sauce*
pinch of ground ginger	*pinch of ground ginger*
4 tablespoons water	*4 tablespoons water*
salt and pepper	*salt and pepper*

Heat the oil in a frying pan and fry the pork chops quickly on each side until browned. Remove from the pan and place in a casserole. Gently fry the onion in the fat remaining in the pan for about 10 minutes, then add the remaining ingredients and bring to the boil. Pour over the chops in the casserole, cover and cook in a moderate oven, 180°C, 350°F, Gas Mark 4 for 1 hour. Taste and adjust the seasoning before serving. **Serves 4**

Pork Belly with Spinach

METRIC/IMPERIAL	AMERICAN
800 g./2 lb. spinach	*2 lb. spinach*
salt and freshly ground black pepper	*salt and freshly ground black pepper*
25 g./1 oz. butter	*2 tablespoons butter*
1 large onion, sliced	*1 large onion, sliced*
400 to 600 g./1 to 1½ lb. potatoes, parboiled for 10 minutes and sliced	*1 to 1½ lb. potatoes, parboiled for 10 minutes and sliced*
400 g./1 lb. pork belly rashers	*1 lb. lean unsmoked bacon slices*

Wash the spinach well in cold water. Bring ¾ cm./¼ in. salted water to the boil in a large pan. Add the spinach and cook for about 8 minutes or until just tender. Drain, chop and season with pepper.

Melt the butter in a frying pan and fry the onion gently for about 5 minutes. Lay the potatoes in a wide, shallow casserole. Top with the onions and cover with the spinach. Lay the pork belly rashers (bacon slices) on the top. Cover and cook in a moderately hot oven, 190°C, 375°F, Gas Mark 5 for 1 hour. Uncover and cook for 30 minutes longer. **Serves 4**

Porkers Hotpot

METRIC/IMPERIAL
25 g./1 oz. lard or dripping
300 g./12 oz. pork belly, thinly sliced
300 g./12 oz. pig's liver, thinly sliced
1 large onion, chopped
2 large carrots, chopped
3 celery stalks, chopped
25 g./1 oz. flour
375 ml./¾ pint stock
¼ teaspoon dried sage
salt and pepper

For the topping:
200 g./8 oz. flour
2 teaspoons baking powder
pinch of salt
50 g./2 oz. butter or margarine
about 6 tablespoons milk

AMERICAN
2 tablespoons lard or dripping
12 oz. fatty unsmoked bacon slices
12 oz. pig's liver, thinly sliced
1 large onion, chopped
2 large carrots, chopped
3 celery stalks, chopped
¼ cup flour
2 cups stock
¼ teaspoon dried sage
salt and pepper

For the topping:
2 cups flour
2 teaspoons baking powder
pinch of salt
¼ cup butter or margarine
about 6 tablespoons milk

Melt the lard or dripping in a large frying pan and fry the pork belly (bacon) on both sides until golden. Remove from the pan with a slotted spoon and place in a casserole. Add the liver to the pan and fry on each side for 2 minutes. Remove from the pan and place in the casserole. Fry the vegetables gently in the fat remaining in the pan for 10 minutes. Sprinkle over the flour and cook for a further 3 minutes, then gradually stir in the stock and bring to the boil, stirring all the time. Add the sage and seasoning and pour into the casserole. Stir gently, cover and cook in a moderate oven, 180°C, 350°F, Gas Mark 4 for 1 hour.

For the topping, sift together the flour, baking powder and salt. Rub in the butter or margarine until the mixture resembles fine breadcrumbs, then bind with the milk to give a soft but not sticky dough. Roll out the dough on a lightly floured surface until it is about 1 cm./½ in. thick and cut into circles with a 5 cm./2 in. cutter.

Remove the casserole from the oven, taste and adjust the seasoning and increase the oven temperature to moderately hot, 200°C, 400°F, Gas Mark 6. Arrange the circles of dough attractively on top of the meat. Brush lightly with milk and replace it in the oven to cook for 20 minutes, or until the scone topping is well risen and golden brown. **Serves 4 to 6**

Note: *While the topping can be frozen it can become rather soggy, so I would advise adding this when reheating.*

Somerset Pork

METRIC/IMPERIAL
600 g./1½ lb. lean pork
50 g./2 oz. flour
salt and pepper
50 g./2 oz. lard or dripping
2 onions, chopped
2 celery stalks, chopped
500 ml./1 pint cider
125 ml./¼ pint single cream

AMERICAN
1½ lb. lean pork
½ cup flour
salt and pepper
¼ cup lard or dripping
2 onions, chopped
2 celery stalks, chopped
2½ cups cider
⅝ cup light cream

Cut the meat into 3¾ cm./1½ in. cubes and coat with the flour, seasoned with salt and pepper. Melt the lard or dripping in a large pan and fry the onions and celery for 5 minutes. Remove from the pan with a slotted spoon and place in a casserole. Add the meat and fry for a further 5 to 10 minutes or until the meat is pale golden on all sides. Gradually stir in the cider and bring to the boil, stirring all the time. Pour into the casserole, cover and cook in a moderate oven, 180°C, 350°C, Gas Mark 4 for 1½ hours. Remove the casserole from the oven, allow to cool slightly, then stir in the cream. Taste and adjust the seasoning before serving. **Serves 4**

Note: *If wishing to deep freeze this dish, do not add the cream before freezing. Reheat and stir in the cream just before serving.*

Pork Chop Casserole

METRIC/IMPERIAL
25 g./1 oz. dripping
4 pork chops (loin or spare rib)
396 g./14 oz. can tomatoes
447 g./15¾ oz. can baked beans
1 onion, chopped
600 g./1½ lb. potatoes, thinly sliced
salt and pepper
¼ teaspoon dried mixed herbs

AMERICAN
2 tablespoons dripping
4 pork chops (loin or spare rib)
14 oz. can tomatoes
15¾ oz. can baked beans
1 onion, chopped
1½ lb. potatoes, thinly sliced
salt and pepper
¼ teaspoon dried mixed herbs

Heat the dripping in a frying pan and fry the pork chops on each side for 5 minutes. Put half the tomatoes, with the juice from the can, baked beans, onion and potatoes in layers in a casserole. Season with salt and pepper and sprinkle with half the herbs. Lay the pork chops on top, then cover with the remaining ingredients in layers, finishing with the potatoes and seasoning. Cover the casserole and cook in a cool oven, 150°C, 300°F, Gas Mark 2 for 3 hours. **Serves 4**

Chunky Pork Supreme

METRIC/IMPERIAL
25 g./1 oz. butter
2 carrots, sliced
3 celery stalks, chopped
1 small green pepper, seeded and chopped
400 g./1 lb. lean pork, diced
2 × 21 g./12 oz. packets onion sauce mix
500 ml./1 pint milk
1 bay leaf
salt and pepper

AMERICAN
2 tablespoons butter
2 carrots, sliced
3 celery stalks, chopped
1 small green pepper, seeded and chopped
1 lb. lean pork, diced
2 × 12 oz. envelopes onion sauce mix
$2^1/_2$ cups milk
1 bay leaf
salt and pepper

Melt the butter in a flameproof casserole and fry the carrots, celery and green pepper for 2 to 3 minutes. Add the pork and cook for 3 to 4 minutes, stirring frequently. Make up the onion sauce mix with the milk, following the instructions on the packet, then add to the pork with the bay leaf. Mix well, cover and cook in a moderate oven, 180°C, 350°F, Gas Mark 4 for $1^1/_2$ hours. Taste and adjust the seasoning and remove the bay leaf before serving. **Serves 4**

Sweet and Sour Ham with Apricots

This is an ideal recipe for using an automatic timer on the oven because the ingredients require no initial cooking and can be left in the oven for 12 hours before cooking.

METRIC/IMPERIAL
453 g./1 lb. canned ham, cut into cubes
439 g./15½ oz. can apricot halves
1 bunch spring onions, chopped
3 celery stalks, sliced
1 red or green pepper, seeded and chopped
2 tomatoes, quartered and sliced
1 tablespoon vinegar
1 tablespoon soy sauce
1 bay leaf
2 teaspoons cornflour
2 tablespoons water
salt and pepper
1 tablespoon chopped parsley

AMERICAN
1 lb. canned ham, cut into cubes
15½ oz. can apricot halves
1 bunch scallions, chopped
3 celery stalks, sliced
1 red or green pepper, seeded and chopped
2 tomatoes, quartered and sliced
1 tablespoon vinegar
1 tablespoon soy sauce
1 bay leaf
2 teaspoons cornstarch
2 tablespoons water
salt and pepper
1 tablespoon chopped parsley

Put the ham into a flameproof casserole together with any jelly or juice from the can, the apricot halves and their juice, the spring onions (scallions), celery, red or green pepper, tomatoes, vinegar, soy sauce and bay leaf. Cover and cook in a moderate oven, 180°C, 350°F, Gas Mark 4 for 45 minutes.

Blend the cornflour (cornstarch) with the water. Remove the casserole from the oven, place on top of the stove and stir in the blended cornflour (cornstarch). Bring to the boil and boil for 2 minutes or until the liquid is lightly thickened. Taste and adjust the seasoning, remove the bay leaf and sprinkle with parsley. **Serves 4**

Frankfurters with White Cabbage

METRIC/IMPERIAL
800 g./2 lb. white cabbage, finely shredded
salt and pepper
25 g./1 oz. butter
1 large onion, chopped
1 garlic clove, crushed
1 large cooking apple, peeled and grated
4 streaky bacon rashers
8 frankfurters
125 ml./$^1/_4$ pint stock

AMERICAN
2 lb. white cabbage, finely shredded
salt and pepper
2 tablespoons butter
1 large onion, chopped
1 garlic clove, crushed
1 large cooking apple, peeled and grated
4 fatty bacon slices
8 frankfurters
$^5/_8$ cup stock

Cook the cabbage in boiling salted water for 5 minutes, drain well and turn into a bowl. Melt the butter in a frying pan and fry the onion and garlic for 5 minutes. Add to the cabbage with the cooking apple, season with salt and pepper and mix well. Put half the cabbage mixture into a casserole.

Stretch the bacon rashers (slices) on a board with the back of a knife and cut each in half. Wrap a piece of bacon round each frankfurter. Lay the frankfurters on top of the cabbage in the casserole and cover with the remaining cabbage. Pour over the stock. Cover and cook in a moderate oven, 180°C, 350°F, Gas Mark 4 for $1^1/_2$ hours. **Serves 4**

Spiced Bacon Joint

METRIC/IMPERIAL

800 g./2 lb. bacon collar joint, soaked overnight and drained
250 ml./½ pint dry cider
400 g./14 oz. peach halves
1 onion, chopped
1 tablespoon Worcestershire sauce
2 teaspoons made mustard
2 tablespoons Demerara sugar
few cloves
1 tablespoon cornflour
2 tablespoons water
1 tablespoon vinegar
salt and freshly ground black pepper

AMERICAN

2 lb. smoked picnic shoulder of pork, soaked overnight and drained
1¼ cups dry cider
14 oz. can peach halves
1 onion, chopped
1 tablespoon Worcestershire sauce
2 teaspoons made mustard
2 tablespoons light brown sugar
few cloves
1 tablespoon cornstarch
2 tablespoons water
1 tablespoon vinegar
salt and freshly ground black pepper

Put the bacon (pork) into a casserole with the cider, the syrup from the peach halves, the onion and Worcestershire sauce. Cover and cook in a moderate oven, 180°C, 350°F, Gas Mark 4 for 1¼ hours.

Increase the oven temperature to hot, 220°C, 425°F, Gas Mark 7. Peel off the skin of the bacon (pork) and cut the fat into diamonds with a sharp knife. Spread the mustard over the fat, sprinkle with the sugar and stick cloves into the diamonds. Replace the joint in the casserole, with the fat uppermost, return to the oven and cook uncovered for 15 minutes or until the fat is crisp and golden brown. Add the peach halves to the juice in the casserole for the last 5 minutes.

Place the bacon (pork) and the peach halves on a heated serving dish and keep warm. Blend the cornflour (cornstarch) with the water in a small saucepan. Strain in the juices from the casserole and add the vinegar. Bring to the boil, stirring all the time until the sauce thickens. Taste and adjust the seasoning and serve this sauce with the bacon (pork) and peaches.

Serves 6 to 8

Bacon, Onion and Potato Casserole

METRIC/IMPERIAL

800 g./2 lb. piece lean flank bacon
800 g./2 lb. potatoes, thinly sliced
400 g./1 lb. onions, thinly sliced
1 large cooking apple, peeled, cored and sliced
½ teaspoon dried sage
salt and freshly ground black pepper
125 ml./¼ pint water
25 g./1 oz. butter

AMERICAN

2 lb. piece lean flank bacon
2 lb. potatoes, thinly sliced
1 lb. onions, thinly sliced
1 large cooking apple, peeled, cored and sliced
½ teaspoon dried sage
salt and freshly ground black pepper
⅝ cup water
2 tablespoons butter

Soak the bacon overnight in cold water. Drain, cut off the rind, then cut into slices. Put layers of potatoes, onions, apple and bacon into a casserole, sprinkling each layer with a very little sage and seasoning and finishing with a layer of potatoes. Pour the water over the top, cover and cook in a warm oven, 170°C, 325°F, Gas Mark 3 for 2 hours. Dot the potatoes with the butter and bake uncovered for a further 30 minutes to brown them.

Serves 6

Sausage, Tomato and Macaroni Layer Casserole

METRIC/IMPERIAL

400 g./1 lb. pork sausages
1 large onion, chopped
1 garlic clove, crushed
425 g./15 oz. can tomatoes
½ teaspoon dried mixed herbs
salt and pepper
150 g./6 oz. macaroni
100 g./4 oz. Cheddar cheese, finely grated

AMERICAN

1 lb. pork sausages
1 large onion, chopped
1 garlic clove, crushed
15 oz. can tomatoes
½ teaspoon dried mixed herbs
salt and pepper
1¼ cups macaroni
1 cup finely grated Cheddar cheese

Put the sausages into a frying pan without any fat and cook gently for 20 minutes, turning from time to time. Remove from the heat, cool slightly, then cut into thick slices. Fry the onion and garlic in the fat remaining in the pan for 5 minutes, then add the tomatoes, with the juice from the can, herbs and seasoning. Bring to the boil and simmer gently for 5 minutes.

Cook the macaroni in a large pan of boiling salted water, following the instructions on the packet (the length of cooking time will depend on the kind of macaroni used). Drain well. Put half the sausage slices in an ovenproof dish, top with half the tomato mixture, half the macaroni and half the cheese. Repeat these layers, sprinkling the remaining cheese on top. Bake uncovered in a moderately hot oven, 200°C, 400°F, Gas Mark 6 for 45 minutes.

Serves 4

Cannelloni with Ham and Mushrooms

METRIC/IMPERIAL
200 g./8 oz. cannelloni
salt

For the filling:
200 g./8 oz. mushrooms, finely chopped
200 g./8 oz. cooked ham, diced
1 onion, finely chopped
2 tablespoons olive oil
2 tablespoons grated Parmesan cheese
salt and pepper

For the cheese sauce:
40 g./1½ oz. butter
40 g./1½ oz. flour
375 ml./¾ pint milk
5 tablespoons grated Parmesan cheese
salt and pepper

AMERICAN
8 oz. cannelloni
salt

For the filling:
8 oz. mushrooms, finely chopped
8 oz. cooked ham, diced
1 onion, finely chopped
2 tablespoons olive oil
2 tablespoons grated Parmesan cheese
salt and pepper

For the cheese sauce:
3 tablespoons butter
6 tablespoons flour
2 cups milk
5 tablespoons grated Parmesan cheese
salt and pepper

Cook the cannelloni in a large pan of boiling salted water for 10 minutes. Drain, rinse in cold water and place on a clean, damp towel to dry.

To make the filling, gently fry the mushrooms, ham and onion in the oil for about 8 minutes. Allow to cool, then add the cheese and seasoning to taste. Stuff this mixture into the cooked and cooled cannelloni using a teaspoon.

To make the cheese sauce, melt the butter in a small pan. Add the flour and cook for 1 minute. Gradually stir in the milk and bring to the boil, stirring all the time until the mixture thickens. Add 3 tablespoons of the cheese and season to taste with salt and pepper. Pour half the cheese sauce into the bottom of a shallow casserole. Top with the stuffed cannelloni, then pour over the remaining cheese sauce. Sprinkle with the remaining Parmesan cheese and cook in a moderately hot oven, 190°C, 375°F, Gas Mark 5 for 30 minutes. **Serves 4**

Creamed Kidneys

METRIC/IMPERIAL
50 g./2 oz. butter
1 green pepper, seeded and sliced
1 red pepper, seeded and sliced
4 pigs' kidneys, skinned, cored, and sliced
15 g./½ oz. flour
salt and pepper
125 ml./¼ pint water
3 tablespoons dry sherry
125 ml./¼ pint single cream

AMERICAN
¼ cup butter
1 green pepper, seeded and sliced
1 red pepper, seeded and sliced
4 pigs' kidneys, skinned, cored, and sliced
2 tablespoons flour
salt and pepper
⅝ cup water
3 tablespoons dry sherry
⅝ cup light cream

Melt the butter in a pan and lightly fry the green and red peppers for 2 to 3 minutes over a moderate heat. Remove from the pan and place in a casserole. Coat the pigs' kidneys with the flour, seasoned with salt and pepper. Fry in the butter remaining in the pan for about 5 minutes. Gradually blend in the water and sherry and bring to the boil. Add to the peppers in the casserole and mix well. Cover and cook in a moderate oven, 180°C, 350°F, Gas Mark 4 for 45 minutes. Stir in the cream and cook for a further 5 minutes, then taste and adjust the seasoning. Serve with boiled rice. **Serves 4**

Note: *If wishing to deep freeze this dish, do not add the cream before freezing. Reheat and stir in the cream just before serving.*

Country Style Liver

METRIC/IMPERIAL
400 to 600 g./1 to 1½ lb. liver, sliced
25 g./1 oz. butter
2 tablespoons olive oil
25 g./1 oz. flour
125 ml./¼ pint water
250 ml./½ pint white wine or cider
1 parsley sprig
salt and pepper
400 g./1 lb. young carrots, sliced lengthways
200 g./8 oz. button onions

To garnish:
1 tablespoon chopped parsley

AMERICAN
1 to 1½ lb. liver, sliced
2 tablespoons butter
2 tablespoons olive oil
¼ cup flour
⅝ cup water
1¼ cups white wine or cider
1 parsley sprig
salt and pepper
1 lb. young carrots, sliced lengthways
8 oz. button onions

To garnish:
1 tablespoon chopped parsley

Fry the liver in the butter and oil in a frying pan for about 2 to 3 minutes on each side. Remove from the pan and place in a casserole. Stir the flour into the fat remaining in the pan and cook over a low heat, stirring, until the flour is dark brown, but not burnt. Add the water, wine or cider, parsley and seasoning and bring to the boil, stirring all the time. Pour over the liver in the casserole. Add the carrots, cover the casserole and cook in a warm oven, 170°C, 325°F, Gas Mark 3 for 1½ hours.

Add the onions to the casserole and cook for a further 1 hour. Taste and adjust the seasoning before serving, sprinkled with chopped parsley.

Serves 4

Liver and Bacon Provençale

METRIC/IMPERIAL
400 g./1 lb. lamb's liver, sliced
50 g./2 oz. flour
salt and pepper
2 tablespoons oil
200 g./8 oz. streaky bacon, chopped
2 large onions, chopped
425 g./15 oz. can tomatoes
½ teaspoon dried marjoram
1 bay leaf
1 tablespoon Worcestershire sauce
375 ml./¾ pint stock

AMERICAN
1 lb. lamb's liver, sliced
½ cup flour
salt and pepper
2 tablespoons oil
8 oz. fatty bacon, chopped
2 large onions, chopped
15 oz. can tomatoes
½ teaspoon dried marjoram
1 bay leaf
1 tablespoon Worcestershire sauce
2 cups stock

Coat the liver with the flour, seasoned with salt and pepper. Heat the oil in a frying pan and fry the liver for about 3 minutes on each side or until golden brown. Remove from the pan and place in a casserole. Fry the bacon and onions in the fat remaining in the pan until golden. Stir in any remaining flour. Add the tomatoes, with the juice from the can, the marjoram, bay leaf and Worcestershire sauce. Stir in the stock, then pour over the liver in the casserole and mix well. Cover and cook in a cool oven, 150°C, 300°F, Gas Mark 2 for 1½ hours. Taste and adjust the seasoning and remove the bay leaf before serving.

Serves 4

Liver Ragoût Sicilienne

METRIC/IMPERIAL
400g./1 lb. ox liver
25 g./1 oz. flour
salt and pepper
50 g./2 oz. dripping
2 large onions, sliced
2 garlic cloves, crushed
250 ml./½ pint stock, or water and ½ stock cube
125 ml./¼ pint cider
1 tablespoon redcurrant jelly
½ teaspoon grated lemon rind
8 stuffed olives

AMERICAN
1 lb. ox liver
¼ cup flour
salt and pepper
¼ cup dripping
2 large onions, sliced
2 garlic cloves, crushed
1¼ cups stock, or water and ½ stock cube
⅝ cup cider
1 tablespoon redcurrant jelly
½ teaspoon grated lemon rind
8 stuffed olives

Cut the liver into narrow strips and coat with the flour, seasoned with salt and pepper. Heat the dripping in a large frying pan, add the liver and cook quickly on all sides for a few minutes. Remove from the pan and place in a casserole. Add the onions and garlic and fry gently for 5 minutes. Sprinkle over any remaining flour and cook for 1 minute. Gradually blend in the stock or water and stock cube and cider and bring to the boil, stirring all the time. Add the redcurrant jelly and lemon rind, pour over the liver in the casserole and cover tightly with a lid.

Cook in a warm oven, 170°C, 325°F, Gas Mark 3 for 30 minutes. Just before serving, stir in the olives. **Serves 4**

Liver, Onion and Apple Casserole

I have suggested using lamb's liver for this recipe but for a cheaper dish you could use ox liver if you do not find it too strong. In this case double the cooking time.

METRIC/IMPERIAL	AMERICAN
50 g./2 oz. dripping	*1/4 cup dripping*
400 g./1 lb. lamb's liver, sliced	*1 lb. lamb's liver, sliced*
2 onions, sliced	*2 onions, sliced*
1 large cooking apple, peeled, cored and chopped	*1 large cooking apple, peeled, cored and chopped*
25 g./1 oz. flour	*1/4 cup flour*
375 ml./3/4 pint stock	*2 cups stock*
1/4 teaspoon dried rosemary	*1/4 teaspoon dried rosemary*
salt and pepper	*salt and pepper*

Heat the dripping in a frying pan and quickly fry the liver for 2 minutes on each side. Remove from the pan with a fish slice or spatula and place in a casserole. Add the onions to the pan and cook for about 5 minutes, then add the apple and cook for a further 5 minutes. Stir in the flour and cook for 1 minute, then gradually stir in the stock and bring to the boil, stirring all the time. Add the rosemary and seasoning and pour into the casserole. Cover and cook in a moderate oven, 180°C, 350°F, Gas Mark 4 for 45 minutes. Taste and adjust the seasoning before serving. **Serves 4**

Devilled Ox Kidney

METRIC/IMPERIAL	AMERICAN
400 g./1 lb. ox kidney	*1 lb. ox kidney*
25 g./1 oz. dripping	*2 tablespoons dripping*
2 large onions, chopped	*2 large onions, chopped*
25 g./1 oz. flour	*1/4 cup flour*
salt and pepper	*salt and pepper*
375 ml./3/4 pint stock	*2 cups stock*
2 teaspoons French mustard	*2 teaspoons French mustard*
1 tablespoon Worcestershire sauce	*1 tablespoon Worcestershire sauce*

Remove the skin of the kidney and soak in a bowl of warm, lightly salted water for about 2 hours. This removes some of the very strong taste of the kidney. Drain and dry well, then cut into 1 cm./1/2 in. thick slices.

Melt the dripping in a frying pan and fry the onions for 5 minutes. Remove from the pan with a slotted spoon and place in a casserole. Coat the kidney with the flour, seasoned with salt and pepper. Add to the pan and fry for about 2 minutes on each side. Transfer to the casserole. Add the stock to the pan and bring to the boil, stirring all the time. Add the mustard and Worcestershire sauce and pour into the casserole. Cover and cook in a warm oven, 170°C, 325°F, Gas Mark 3 for 1 1/2 hours. Taste and adjust the seasoning before serving. **Serves 4**

Creamed Sweetbreads Casserole

METRIC/IMPERIAL	AMERICAN
400 g./1 lb. sweetbreads, either lambs' or calves'	*1 lb. sweetbreads, either lambs' or calves'*
salt and pepper	*salt and pepper*
50 g./2 oz. butter	*1/4 cup butter*
1 onion, chopped	*1 onion, chopped*
25 g./1 oz. flour	*1/4 cup flour*
250 ml./1/2 pint stock	*1 1/4 cups stock*
1/2 teaspoon dried mixed herbs	*1/2 teaspoon dried mixed herbs*
200 g./8 oz. fresh shelled or frozen peas	*8 oz. fresh shelled or frozen peas*
100 g./4 oz. button mushrooms, sliced	*4 oz. button mushrooms, sliced*
1 tablespoon lemon juice	*1 tablespoon lemon juice*
125 ml./1/4 pint single cream	*5/8 cup light cream*

Soak the sweetbreads for about 1 hour in cold, salted water to remove the blood. Drain, put into a saucepan and cover with fresh cold water. Bring slowly to the boil, then drain again.

Melt the butter in a flameproof casserole, add the onion and cook gently for 5 minutes. Stir in the flour and cook for 1 minute, then gradually stir in the stock and bring to the boil, stirring all the time. Add the sweetbreads and herbs and season to taste. Cover and cook in a warm oven, 170°C, 325°F, Gas Mark 3 for 1 1/2 hours.

Add the peas and mushrooms and continue cooking for a further 30 minutes. Stir in the lemon juice and the cream and taste and adjust the seasoning before serving. **Serves 4**

Note: *If wishing to deep freeze this dish, do not add the cream before freezing. Reheat and stir in the cream just before serving.*

Oxtail with Grapes ►

In both this and the recipe for Oxtail with Black Olives it is best if you can make the dish the day before, leave it to cool, and then refrigerate it overnight so that all the excess fat can easily be removed from the top.

METRIC/IMPERIAL	AMERICAN
2 medium-sized to large oxtails, cut in 5 cm./2 in. pieces	*2 medium-sized to large oxtails, cut in 2 in. pieces*
4 to 5 streaky bacon rashers, chopped	*4 to 5 fatty bacon slices, chopped*
2 large onions, chopped	*2 large onions, chopped*
2 garlic cloves, crushed	*2 garlic cloves, crushed*
4 large carrots, sliced	*4 large carrots, sliced*
2 bay leaves	*2 bay leaves*
1 parsley sprig	*1 parsley sprig*
1 thyme sprig	*1 thyme sprig*
salt and pepper	*salt and pepper*
800 g./2 lb. seedless white grapes	*2 lb. seedless white grapes*

Cut off any excess fat from the oxtails and soak them for about 3 hours in cold water to allow the blood to drain out. Drain and dry well.

Fry the bacon in a large flameproof casserole over a gentle heat until the fat runs out. Add the onions, garlic and carrots and fry gently, stirring a few times, for about 10 minutes. Add the oxtail, together with the bay leaves, parsley, thyme and seasoning and cook for a further 20 minutes, stirring from time to time. Take the grapes off the stalks and crush them lightly in a bowl. Add to the casserole, cover with a sheet of foil, then the lid and transfer to a cool oven, 150°C, 300°F, Gas Mark 2 to cook for 4 hours.

Remove from the oven, allow to cool, then skim off all the excess fat. Take all the meat off the bones and place in a casserole or saucepan with the carrots. Push the sauce through a strainer or put into a liquidizer and blend for a minute, then pour over the meat. Reheat gently either on top of the stove or in a moderate oven, 180°C, 350°F, Gas Mark 4 for 35 to 45 minutes. Skim off all excess fat before serving. **Serves 8**

Oxtail with Black Olives

METRIC/IMPERIAL	AMERICAN
2 medium-sized oxtails, cut in 5 cm./2 in. pieces	*2 medium-sized oxtails, cut in 2 in. pieces*
2 tablespoons olive oil	*2 tablespoons olive oil*
4 tablespoons brandy	*4 tablespoons brandy*
250 ml./1/2 pint white wine	*1 1/4 cups white wine*
stock or water	*stock or water*
2 garlic cloves, crushed	*2 garlic cloves, crushed*
finely pared rind of 1/2 small orange	*finely pared rind of 1/2 small orange*
1 bouquet garni	*1 bouquet garni*
100 g./4 oz. black olives, stoned	*4 oz. black olives, pitted*
25 g./1 oz. butter	*2 tablespoons butter*
25 g./1 oz. flour	*1/4 cup flour*

Cut off any excess fat from the oxtails and soak them for about 3 hours in cold water to allow the blood to drain out. Drain and dry well.

Heat the oil in a large flameproof casserole, add a few pieces of oxtail at a time and fry until brown all over. Return all the oxtail to the casserole. Warm the brandy in a small pan, ignite and pour over the oxtail. Do this very carefully as the flames can leap quite high. When the flames have died down, add the wine and let it boil rapidly for a few minutes. Add just enough stock or water to cover the oxtail, with the garlic, orange rind and bouquet garni. Cover the casserole and cook in a cool oven, 150°C, 300°F, Gas Mark 2 for 3 hours. Pour the liquid off into a bowl, discard the orange rind and bouquet garni and refrigerate the liquid and meat separately overnight.

The following day, skim off all the excess fat from the liquid. Turn into a pan with the oxtail and the olives and cook on top of the stove for a further 1 to 1 1/2 hours or until the meat comes easily away from the bones. Blend the butter and flour together until they form a smooth paste. Add to the simmering liquid a teaspoon at a time, stirring well between each addition. Allow to simmer for a further 5 minutes, then serve with boiled rice. **Serves 8**

Poultry & Game Casseroles

There are two very good points in favour of casseroling poultry; first, long, slow cooking with herbs and spices adds flavour to today's rather flavourless battery chickens, and second, it enables you to make use of boiling chickens which are usually cheaper and have more flavour. Apart from one recipe, I have assumed that most people will be using chicken joints (pieces) or younger roasting chicken, but boiling chicken can always be used provided that the cooking time is increased by about 2 hours.

Some people feel that it is a sacrilege to casserole a game bird and, particularly if one is not lucky enough to eat game very often, nothing is nicer than a roasted pheasant or grouse. However, if the bird is of dubious age I think it is better to serve it tender in a casserole than roasted and tough. It is sometimes possible to buy game birds which are sold specifically for casseroling and these are much cheaper than the roasting birds.

Chicken Curry with Yogurt

METRIC/IMPERIAL	AMERICAN
4 chicken breasts	*4 chicken breasts*
1 teaspoon ground turmeric	*1 teaspoon ground turmeric*
1 teaspoon ground cumin	*1 teaspoon ground cumin*
1 garlic clove, crushed	*1 garlic clove, crushed*
250 ml./½ pint natural yogurt	*1¼ cups natural yogurt*
25 g./1 oz. butter	*2 tablespoons butter*
1 onion, sliced	*1 onion, sliced*
¼ teaspoon ground cloves	*¼ teaspoon ground cloves*
1 teaspoon ground cinnamon	*1 teaspoon ground cinnamon*
salt	*salt*

Remove the skin and bone from the chicken breasts, cut into bite-sized pieces and place in a shallow dish. Blend the turmeric, cumin, garlic and two-thirds of the yogurt together. Pour over the chicken and leave to marinate for 1 hour.

Melt the butter in a flameproof casserole and gently fry the onion for 5 minutes until golden. Add the cloves and cinnamon and fry for a further 2 to 3 minutes. Add the meat together with the marinade and a little salt. Cover and cook in a warm oven, 170°C, 325°F, Gas Mark 3 for 1½ hours. Stir in the extra yogurt just before serving and taste and adjust the seasoning. **Serves 4**

Note: *Do not deep freeze this dish.*

Chicken and Peanut Casserole

METRIC/IMPERIAL	AMERICAN
1¼ kg./3 lb. chicken	*3 lb. chicken*
50 g./2 oz. butter	*¼ cup butter*
1 onion, chopped	*1 onion, chopped*
25 g./1 oz. flour	*¼ cup flour*
3 tablespoons crunchy peanut butter	*3 tablespoons crunchy peanut butter*
375 ml./¾ pint milk	*2 cups milk*
salt and pepper	*salt and pepper*
50 g./2 oz. salted peanuts	*¼ cup salted peanuts*
25 g./1 oz. fresh white breadcrumbs	*½ cup fresh white breadcrumbs*

Cut the chicken into joints (pieces). Melt the butter in a large pan and fry the chicken on all sides until golden brown. Remove from the pan and place in a casserole. Add the onion to the pan and cook for 5 minutes. Stir in the flour and cook for 2 minutes, then remove from the heat and stir in the peanut butter and milk. Return to the heat and bring to the boil, stirring all the time. Season and pour over the chicken in the casserole. Cover and cook in a moderately hot oven, 190°C, 375°F, Gas Mark 5 for 1 hour. Remove the lid, sprinkle with the peanuts and breadcrumbs and bake uncovered for a further 10 minutes. **Serves 4 to 6**

Note: *If wishing to deep freeze this dish, do not add the topping until reheating.*

Chicken with Apricots

METRIC/IMPERIAL
200 g./8 oz. dried apricots
25 g./1 oz. butter
2 tablespoons oil
1¼ kg./3 lb. chicken, cut into serving pieces
1 onion, chopped
25 g./1 oz. flour
salt and pepper
1 bouquet garni
sugar (optional)
1 parsley sprig

AMERICAN
1⅓ cups dried apricots
2 tablespoons butter
2 tablespoons oil
3 lb. chicken, cut into serving pieces
1 onion, chopped
¼ cup flour
salt and pepper
1 bouquet garni
sugar (optional)
1 parsley sprig

Cover the apricots with cold water and leave to soak overnight. Drain, reserving the soaking liquid. Make it up to 500 ml./1 pint (2½ cups) with water, if necessary. Heat the butter and oil in a pan. Fry the chicken pieces on all sides until golden brown. Remove from the pan and place in a casserole. Fry the onion in the fat remaining in the pan for 5 minutes. Sprinkle in the flour and cook for 2 minutes, stirring constantly. Gradually stir in the apricot liquid, then bring to the boil, stirring all the time. Add the apricots, seasoning and bouquet garni. Pour over the chicken in the casserole. Cover and cook in a moderate oven, 180°C, 350°F, Gas Mark 4 for 1 hour. Taste and adjust the seasoning and remove the bouquet garni. Add a little sugar if wished, and serve garnished with parsley.

Serves 6

Mild Chicken Curry

METRIC/IMPERIAL
1¼ kg./3 lb. chicken
4 tablespoons oil
2 onions, chopped
25 g./1 oz. flour
1 tablespoon curry powder
250 ml./½ pint chicken stock, or water and 1 chicken stock cube
1 tablespoon mango chutney
1 tablespoon cherry jam
salt and pepper
2 tablespoons sultanas
1 dessert apple, cored and chopped
few lemon wedges

AMERICAN
3 lb. chicken
4 tablespoons oil
2 onions, chopped
¼ cup flour
1 tablespoon curry powder
1¼ cups chicken stock, or water and 1 chicken stock cube
1 tablespoon mango chutney
1 tablespoon cherry jam
salt and pepper
2 tablespoons seedless raisins
1 dessert apple, cored and chopped
few lemon wedges

Cut the chicken into eight pieces. Heat the oil in a large frying pan, add the chicken pieces and fry until golden brown on all sides. Remove from the pan and place in a casserole. Fry the onions in the oil remaining in the pan until soft. Blend in the flour and curry powder and cook for 1 minute. Gradually add the stock, or water and stock cube, then bring to the boil, stirring all the time. Add the chutney, jam and seasoning and pour over the chicken in the casserole. Cover and cook in a warm oven, 170°C, 325°F, Gas Mark 3 for 45 minutes.

Add the sultanas (raisins) and apple and cook, covered, for a further 30 minutes. Taste and adjust the seasoning. Garnish with lemon wedges and serve with boiled rice, poppadums, peanuts, wedges of hard-boiled egg and chopped cucumber and tomato. **Serves 4**

Chicken Paprika

METRIC/IMPERIAL
50 g./2 oz. butter
2 tablespoons oil
4 chicken joints
25 g./1 oz. flour
2 tablespoons paprika
500 ml./1 pint chicken stock, or water and 1 chicken stock cube
2 tablespoons redcurrant jelly
finely pared rind of 1 lemon
1 thyme sprig
1 parsley sprig
100 g./4 oz. button mushrooms
125 ml./¼ pint soured cream

AMERICAN
¼ cup butter
2 tablespoons oil
4 chicken pieces
¼ cup flour
2 tablespoons paprika
2½ cups chicken stock, or water and 1 chicken stock cube
2 tablespoons redcurrant jelly
finely pared rind of 1 lemon
1 thyme sprig
1 parsley sprig
4 oz. button mushrooms
⅝ cup sour cream

Heat the butter and oil in a frying pan and fry the chicken joints (pieces) on all sides until golden brown. Remove from the pan and place in a casserole. Stir the flour and paprika into the fat remaining in the pan and cook gently for 2 to 3 minutes. Gradually stir in the stock or water and stock cube and the redcurrant jelly and bring to the boil, stirring all the time. Pour over the chicken in the casserole. Tie the lemon rind, thyme and parsley together with a piece of thread and add to the chicken with the mushrooms. Cover and cook in a moderate oven, 180°C, 350°F, Gas Mark 4 for 1½ hours.

Remove the lemon rind, thyme and parsley. Taste and adjust the seasoning and pile the soured cream in the centre just before serving. **Serves 4**

Note: *If wishing to freeze, do not add the soured cream. Freeze, then reheat and add the soured cream just before serving.*

Chicken and Avocado Casserole

METRIC/IMPERIAL	AMERICAN
6 chicken joints	*6 chicken pieces*
40 g./1½ oz. flour	*6 tablespoons flour*
salt and pepper	*salt and pepper*
1 tablespoon chopped fresh thyme	*1 tablespoon chopped fresh thyme*
grated rind and juice of 1 lemon	*grated rind and juice of 1 lemon*
50 g./2 oz. butter	*¼ cup butter*
2 onions, chopped	*2 onions, chopped*
250 ml./½ pint white wine	*1¼ cups white wine*
125 ml./¼ pint chicken stock	*⅝ cup chicken stock*
125 ml./¼ pint soured cream	*⅝ cup sour cream*
2 avocado pears, peeled, stoned and sliced	*2 avocados, peeled, stoned and sliced*

Coat the chicken joints (pieces) with the flour, seasoned with salt and pepper, the chopped thyme and lemon rind. Melt the butter in a large frying pan and fry the chicken joints (pieces) on all sides until golden brown. Remove from the pan and place in a casserole. Fry the onions in the fat remaining in the pan for about 5 minutes. Sprinkle over any remaining flour, cook for 1 minute, then gradually stir in the wine and stock. Bring to the boil, stirring all the time. Pour over the chicken in the casserole, cover and cook in a moderate oven, 180°C, 350°F, Gas Mark 4 for 1 hour.

Remove the casserole from the oven, allow to cool for a minute, then stir in the soured cream. Toss the avocado slices in the lemon juice. Add to the chicken, cover the casserole and return to the oven for a further 10 minutes. **Serves 6**

Note: *Do not freeze this dish after the cream and avocado pears have been added. If wishing to freeze, cook for 1 hour then freeze. Reheat and then add the soured cream and avocado pears as above.*

Chicken Hot-Pot

METRIC/IMPERIAL
600 g./1½ lb. potatoes, sliced
400 g./1 lb. onions, sliced
300 g./12 oz. tomatoes, peeled and sliced
salt and pepper
4 chicken joints
1 teaspoon chopped fresh rosemary
250 ml./½ pint chicken stock
25 g./1 oz. butter

AMERICAN
1½ lb. potatoes, sliced
1 lb. onions, sliced
12 oz. tomatoes, peeled and sliced
salt and pepper
4 chicken pieces
1 teaspoon chopped fresh rosemary
1¼ cups chicken stock
2 tablespoons butter

Put a layer of potatoes into a casserole, cover with a layer of onions, then tomatoes. Season each layer well with salt and pepper. Lay the chicken joints (pieces) on the vegetables and sprinkle with the rosemary and more seasoning. Cover with the remaining tomatoes, onions and potatoes, seasoning each layer as before. Pour over the stock and dot the potatoes with the butter. Cover and cook in a warm oven, 170°C, 325°F, Gas Mark 3 for 1½ hours. Remove the lid of the casserole and cook for 30 minutes uncovered to brown the potatoes.

Serves 4

Coq au Vin

METRIC/IMPERIAL
1½ kg./3 lb. chicken
40 g./1½ oz. butter
1 tablespoon oil
100 g./4 oz. piece smoked streaky bacon, cubed
12 button onions
2 celery stalks, chopped
150 g./6 oz. button mushrooms
1 garlic clove, crushed
25 g./1 oz. flour
375 ml./¾ pint red wine
125 ml./¼ pint water
1 bay leaf
1 thyme sprig
salt and freshly ground black pepper

AMERICAN
3 lb. chicken
3 tablespoons butter
1 tablespoon oil
4 oz. piece smoked fatty bacon, cubed
12 button onions
2 celery stalks, chopped
6 oz. button mushrooms
1 garlic clove, crushed
¼ cup flour
2 cups red wine
⅝ cup water
1 bay leaf
1 thyme sprig
salt and freshly ground black pepper

Cut the chicken into serving pieces, and reserve the giblets. Melt 25 g./1 oz. (2 tablespoons) of the butter and the oil in a frying pan and fry the bacon cubes until golden brown. Remove from the pan and put into a casserole. Increase the heat and fry the chicken joints in the fat remaining in the pan on all sides until golden brown. Remove from the pan and place in the casserole. Add the onions and celery to the pan and fry for 5 minutes. Transfer to the casserole.

Add the remaining butter to the pan with the mushrooms and fry for 5 minutes. Remove from the pan and put on one side. Add the garlic and flour to the fat remaining in the pan and cook over a gentle heat, stirring frequently, until the flour is browned, but not burnt. Gradually stir in the wine and water and bring to the boil, stirring all the time. Add the bay leaf and thyme, season with salt and pepper and pour over the chicken in the casserole. Add the chicken giblets. Cover and cook in a warm oven, 170°C, 325°F, Gas Mark 3 for 1½ hours.

Remove the bay leaf, thyme and chicken giblets from the casserole and add the mushrooms. Cover and cook for a further 15 minutes. Taste and adjust the seasoning before serving.

Serves 6

Chicken with Barbecue Sauce

METRIC/IMPERIAL
25 g./1 oz. dripping
4 chicken joints
1 large onion, finely chopped
1 garlic clove, crushed
70 g./2¼ oz. can tomato purée
4 tablespoons water
2 tablespoons soft brown sugar
3 tablespoons vinegar
2 teaspoons Worcestershire sauce
1 teaspoon made English mustard
pinch of dried mixed herbs
salt and pepper

AMERICAN
2 tablespoons dripping
4 chicken pieces
1 large onion, finely chopped
1 garlic clove, crushed
2¼ oz. can tomato purée
4 tablespoons water
2 tablespoons soft brown sugar
3 tablespoons vinegar
2 teaspoons Worcestershire sauce
1 teaspoon made English mustard
pinch of dried mixed herbs
salt and pepper

Melt the dripping in a large pan, add the chicken joints (pieces) and fry for about 8 minutes or until golden brown on all sides. Remove from the pan and place in a casserole. Add the onion and garlic to the fat remaining in the pan and fry gently for 5 minutes. Add all the remaining ingredients, stir and bring almost to the boil. Pour over the chicken in the casserole, cover and cook in a warm oven, 170°C, 325°F, Gas Mark 3 for 1 hour.

Serves 4

Chicken with Apples and Cider

METRIC/IMPERIAL	AMERICAN
200 g./4 oz. butter	*½ cup butter*
1¼ kg./3 lb. chicken, cut into serving pieces	*3 lb. chicken, cut into serving pieces*
6 dessert apples	*6 dessert apples*
salt and freshly ground black pepper	*salt and freshly ground black pepper*
25 g./1 oz. flour	*¼ cup flour*
375 ml./¾ pint cider	*2 cups cider*
1 bouquet garni	*1 bouquet garni*
3 tablespoons water	*3 tablespoons water*
125 ml./¼ pint double cream	*⅝ cup heavy cream*
1 tablespoon chopped parsley	*1 tablespoon chopped parsley*

Melt half the butter in a flameproof casserole, add the chicken and fry until golden brown on all sides. Remove from the pan and put on one side. Peel, core and slice two of the apples, sprinkle with salt and pepper and fry in the butter remaining in the casserole until beginning to brown. Sprinkle in the flour and cook gently, stirring occasionally, until the flour is a pale golden brown. Gradually stir in 250 ml./½ pint (1¼ cups) of the cider and bring to the boil, stirring all the time. Replace the chicken in the casserole and add the bouquet garni. Cover and cook in a moderately hot oven, 190°C, 375°F, Gas Mark 5 for 1 hour.

Shortly before the end of the cooking time, peel, core and quarter the remaining apples. Melt half the remaining butter in the frying pan and fry the apples until lightly browned. Put into an ovenproof dish with the water, cover and put into the oven, under the chicken, until required.

When the chicken is cooked, remove it from the casserole, place on a heated serving dish and keep hot. Add the remaining cider to the juices in the casserole and boil rapidly, uncovered, on top of the stove for about 10 minutes or until well reduced. Strain into a clean pan. Add the quartered apples, cream and the rest of the butter, cut into small pieces. Reheat gently without boiling. Taste and adjust the seasoning and pour the sauce over the chicken. Garnish with the chopped parsley.

Serves 6

Chicken with Tomatoes and Olives

METRIC/IMPERIAL
4 chicken joints
25 g./1 oz. flour
salt and pepper
3 tablespoons olive oil
2 onions, chopped
2 garlic cloves, crushed
400 g./1 lb. tomatoes, peeled
200 g./4 oz. mushrooms sliced
100 g./4 oz. olives
1 bouquet garni
pinch of powdered saffron
250 ml./½ pint white wine
juice of 1 lemon
2 tablespoons chopped parsley

AMERICAN
4 chicken pieces
¼ cup flour
salt and pepper
3 tablespoons olive oil
2 onions, chopped
2 garlic cloves, crushed
1 lb. tomatoes, peeled
4 oz. mushrooms, sliced
4 oz. olives
1 bouquet garni
pinch of powdered saffron
1¼ cups white wine
juice of 1 lemon
2 tablespoons chopped parsley

Coat the chicken joints (pieces) with the flour, seasoned with salt and pepper. Heat the oil in a wide, shallow pan and fry the chicken joints for about 8 minutes, or until golden brown all over. Remove from the pan and place in a casserole. Add the onions to the pan and fry for 5 minutes. Add the garlic, tomatoes, mushrooms, olives, bouquet garni, saffron and wine and bring to the boil. Pour over the chicken in the casserole. Cover and cook in a moderate oven, 180°C, 350°F, Gas Mark 4 for 1 hour or until the chicken is tender. Remove the bouquet garni. Stir in the lemon juice and taste and adjust the seasoning. Serve sprinkled with parsley. **Serves 4**

Mushroom-stuffed Poussins ►

METRIC/IMPERIAL	AMERICAN
50 g./2 oz. butter	*¼ cup butter*
1 small onion, finely chopped	*1 small onion, finely chopped*
1 garlic clove, crushed	*1 garlic clove, crushed*
100 g./4 oz. mushrooms, finely chopped	*4 oz. mushrooms, finely chopped*
40 g./1½ oz. fresh white breadcrumbs	*¾ cup fresh white breadcrumbs*
1 teaspoon chopped fresh thyme	*1 teaspoon chopped fresh thyme*
1 tablespoon chopped parsley	*1 tablespoon chopped parsley*
salt and freshly ground black pepper	*salt and freshly ground black pepper*
1 egg yolk	*1 egg yolk*
2 double poussins	*2 double poussins*
1 tablespoon oil	*1 tablespoon oil*
125 ml./¼ pint dry cider or white wine	*⅝ cup dry cider or white wine*
125 ml./¼ pint chicken stock	*⅝ cup chicken stock*

Melt half the butter in a small saucepan, add the onion and garlic and cook gently for 5 minutes. Add the mushrooms and cook for a further 5 minutes. Remove from the heat. Stir in the breadcrumbs, herbs and seasoning and bind with the egg yolk. Use this mixture to stuff the two poussins.

Heat the remaining butter and the oil in a large frying pan and fry the poussins on all sides until golden brown. Transfer the poussins to a casserole. Add the cider or white wine and stock to the juices in the pan, bring to the boil and pour over the poussins in the casserole. Cover and cook in a moderate oven, 180°C, 350°F, Gas Mark 4 for 45 minutes. **Serves 4**

Summer Chicken Casserole

METRIC/IMPERIAL	AMERICAN
25 g./1 oz. butter	*2 tablespoons butter*
1 tablespoon oil	*1 tablespoon oil*
4 chicken joints	*4 chicken pieces*
1 bunch spring onions	*1 bunch scallions*
4 back bacon rashers, chopped	*4 lean bacon slices, chopped*
100 g./4 oz. mushrooms, quartered	*4 oz. mushrooms, quartered*
250 ml./½ pint chicken stock	*1¼ cups chicken stock*
400 g./1 lb. new potatoes, scraped	*1 lb. new potatoes, scraped*
salt and pepper	*salt and pepper*

Heat the butter and oil in a frying pan and fry the chicken joints (pieces) for about 8 minutes or until golden brown on all sides. Remove from the pan and place in a casserole. Finely chop about 2 tablespoons of the spring onion (scallion) tops, but leave the remaining onions whole. Add the whole onions to the fat remaining in the pan with the bacon and mushrooms and fry for 5 minutes. Add to the chicken in the casserole together with the chicken stock and potatoes. Season with salt and pepper. Cover the casserole and cook in a moderate oven, 180°C, 350°F, Gas Mark 4 for 1 hour. Taste and adjust the seasoning and sprinkle with the chopped spring onion (scallion) tops. **Serves 4**

Chicken Marengo

METRIC/IMPERIAL	AMERICAN
1¾ kg./4 lb. chicken	*4 lb. chicken*
50 g./2 oz. butter	*¼ cup butter*
2 tablespoons olive oil	*2 tablespoons olive oil*
4 shallots or 2 small onions, chopped	*4 shallots or 2 small onions, chopped*
25 g./1 oz. flour	*¼ cup flour*
4 tablespoons tomato purée	*4 tablespoons tomato purée*
125 ml./¼ pint dry sherry	*⅝ cup dry sherry*
250 ml./½ pint chicken stock	*1¼ cups chicken stock*
200 g./8 oz. mushrooms	*8 oz. mushrooms*
1 bouquet garni	*1 bouquet garni*
pinch of sugar	*pinch of sugar*
salt and pepper	*salt and pepper*

Cut the chicken into joints (pieces). Heat half the butter and all the oil in a large frying pan and fry the chicken on all sides for about 8 minutes until golden brown. Remove from the pan and place in a casserole. Add the shallots or onions to the pan and cook gently for 5 minutes. Stir in the flour and cook for 1 minute. Add the tomato purée then the sherry and stock and bring to the boil, stirring all the time. Pour over the chicken in the casserole and add the mushroom stalks, bouquet garni, sugar and seasoning. Cover and cook in a moderate oven, 180°C, 350°F, Gas Mark 4 for 1¼ hours.

Just before serving, melt the remaining butter in a frying pan and fry the mushroom caps. Remove the casserole from the oven. Take out the chicken joints (pieces) and arrange on a heated serving dish, then strain the sauce over the chicken. Garnish with the mushroom caps. **Serves 4 to 6**

Chicken and Mushroom Casserole ►

METRIC/IMPERIAL

1¼ kg./3 lb. chicken
25 g./1 oz. butter
300 g./12 oz. button onions
4 celery stalks, cut into pieces
25 g./1 oz. flour
250 ml./½ pint chicken stock
1 bouquet garni
salt and pepper
100 g./4 oz. button mushrooms

AMERICAN

3 lb. chicken
2 tablespoons butter
12 oz. button onions
4 celery stalks, cut into pieces
¼ cup flour
1¼ cups chicken stock
1 bouquet garni
salt and pepper
4 oz. button mushrooms

Cut the chicken into joints (pieces). Melt the butter in a large frying pan and fry the chicken until golden brown. Remove from the pan and place in a casserole. Add the onions and celery to the pan and fry for about 10 minutes, then stir in the flour and cook for a further minute. Gradually stir in the stock and bring to the boil, stirring all the time. Add the bouquet garni and seasoning and pour over the chicken in the casserole. Cover and cook in a moderate oven, 180°C, 350°F, Gas Mark 4 for 45 minutes. Add the mushrooms and cook for a further 15 minutes. Taste and adjust the seasoning. Remove the bouquet garni. Arrange the chicken and vegetables on a heated serving dish with boiled rice, peas and sweetcorn.

Serves 4

Chicken in Almond, Stem Ginger and Yogurt Sauce

METRIC/IMPERIAL

25 g./1 oz. butter
1 tablespoon oil
4 chicken joints
1 onion, chopped
25 g./1 oz. flour
250 ml./½ pint chicken stock
½ teaspoon grated nutmeg
50 g./2 oz. stem ginger, sliced
100 g./4 oz. button mushrooms
salt and pepper
500 ml./1 pint natural yogurt
50 g./2 oz. split almonds

AMERICAN

2 tablespoons butter
1 tablespoon oil
4 chicken pieces
1 onion, chopped
¼ cup flour
1¼ cups chicken stock
½ teaspoon grated nutmeg
⅓ cup sliced stem ginger
4 oz. button mushrooms
salt and pepper
2½ cups natural yogurt
⅓ cup split almonds

Heat the butter and oil in a frying pan. Add the chicken joints (pieces) and fry for about 8 minutes or until golden brown. Remove from the pan and place in a casserole. Add the onion to the pan and cook gently for 5 minutes. Stir in the flour and cook for 2 minutes. Gradually stir in the stock and bring to the boil, stirring all the time. Add the nutmeg, ginger, mushrooms and seasoning and pour over the chicken in the casserole. Cover and cook in a warm oven, 170°C, 325°F, Gas Mark 3 for 1 hour.

Remove the casserole from the oven, allow to cool slightly, then stir in the yogurt. Return to the oven and cook for a further 5 minutes to heat through the yogurt. Meanwhile, lightly toast the almonds under the grill (broiler) until they are golden brown. Taste and adjust the seasoning of the casserole and sprinkle with the almonds before serving. **Serves 4**

Note: *If wishing to deep freeze this dish, do not add the yogurt before freezing. Reheat, stir in the yogurt as above, and sprinkle with almonds just before serving.*

Country Stuffed Chicken

METRIC/IMPERIAL

100 g./4 oz. long grain rice
salt and pepper
25 g./1 oz. raisins
2 celery stalks, finely chopped
25 g./1 oz. butter
1¾ to 2 kg./4 to 5 lb. boiling chicken
400 g./1 lb. carrots
400 g./1 lb. button onions
400 g./1 lb. small tomatoes, peeled
4 tablespoons water

AMERICAN

⅔ cup long grain rice
salt and pepper
3 tablespoons raisins
2 celery stalks, finely chopped
2 tablespoons butter
4 to 5 lb. boiling chicken
1 lb. carrots
1 lb. button onions
1 lb. small tomatoes, peeled
4 tablespoons water

Cook the rice in boiling salted water until just tender. Stir in the raisins, celery and butter and use this mixture to stuff the chicken.

Peel or scrape the carrots. If they are young leave them whole; if they are large, old ones cut into quarters lengthways. Put the vegetables and water in a large casserole and season with salt and pepper. Place the stuffed chicken on top. Cover and cook in a warm oven, 170°C, 325°F, Gas Mark 3 for 3½ to 4 hours or until the chicken is tender. **Serves 6 to 8**

Chicken Casserole with Tomato Dumplings

METRIC/IMPERIAL
4 chicken joints
50 g./2 oz. flour
salt and pepper
50 g./2 oz. butter
8 button onions
2 celery stalks, chopped
2 carrots, sliced
500 ml./1 pint water
½ lemon, thinly sliced
1 bay leaf
100 g./4 oz. frozen peas
125 ml./¼ pint soured cream
1 tablespoon chopped parsley

For the dumplings:
100 g./4 oz. self-raising flour
½ teaspoon salt
40 g./1½ oz. shredded suet
½ teaspoon dried oregano
1 tablespoon tomato purée
3 to 4 tablespoons cold water

AMERICAN
4 chicken pieces
½ cup flour
salt and pepper
¼ cup butter
8 button onions
2 celery stalks, chopped
2 carrots, sliced
2½ cups water
½ lemon, thinly sliced
1 bay leaf
4 oz. frozen peas
⅝ cup sour cream
1 tablespoon chopped parsley

For the dumplings:
1 cup self-rising flour
½ teaspoon salt
3 tablespoons shredded suet
½ teaspoon dried oregano
1 tablespoon tomato purée
3 to 4 tablespoons cold water

Toss the chicken joints (pieces) in the flour, seasoned with salt and pepper. Melt the butter in a large frying pan and fry the chicken joints (pieces) on all sides until golden brown. Remove from the pan with a slotted spoon and place in a casserole. Add the onions, celery and carrots to the pan and cook gently for 5 minutes. Stir in the water and bring to the boil, stirring all the time. Add the lemon, bay leaf and seasoning and pour over the chicken in the casserole. Cover and cook in a moderate oven, 180°C, 350°F, Gas Mark 4 for 1¼ hours. Stir in the peas and cook for a further 15 minutes.

For the dumplings, sift together the flour and salt. Add the suet and oregano. Blend the tomato purée with the water and stir into the flour mixture to form a soft but not sticky dough. Turn on to a floured surface and knead for 1 minute. Divide the dumplings into eight balls with floured hands. Cook gently in simmering salted water for 20 minutes.

Just before serving remove the casserole from the oven, allow to cool slightly, then stir in the soured cream. Place the dumplings on top and sprinkle with parsley. **Serves 4**

Note: *If wishing to deep freeze this dish, add the dumplings, but not the cream, then freeze. Reheat and stir in the cream just before serving.*

Turkey and Ham Medley

METRIC/IMPERIAL
150 g./6 oz. raw smoked or cooked sliced ham
200 g./8 oz. cooked turkey or chicken
3 tablespoons oil, preferably olive
2 celery stalks, chopped
40 g./1½ oz. flour
375 ml./¾ pint milk
150 g./6 oz. Cheddar or Edam cheese, grated
1 teaspoon made mustard
2 teaspoons vinegar
egg yolk (optional)
salt and freshly ground black pepper

AMERICAN
6 oz. raw smoked or cooked sliced ham
8 oz. cooked turkey or chicken
3 tablespoons oil, preferably olive
2 celery stalks, chopped
6 tablespoons flour
2 cups milk
1½ cups grated Cheddar or Edam cheese
1 teaspoon made mustard
2 teaspoons vinegar
egg yolk (optional)
salt and freshly ground black pepper

Lay half the slices of ham in a casserole. Break the turkey or chicken into small pieces on top and cover with the remaining ham. Heat the oil in a saucepan, add the celery and cook gently for 10 minutes. Stir in the flour and cook for 2 minutes. Gradually stir in the milk and bring to the boil, stirring all the time. Remove from the heat and stir in almost all the cheese, the mustard, vinegar, egg yolk, if using, and seasoning. Pour over the meat in the casserole and sprinkle with the remaining cheese.

Cook, uncovered, in a moderately hot oven, 190°C, 375°F, Gas Mark 5 for 40 minutes or until heated through and golden brown.

Serves 4 to 6

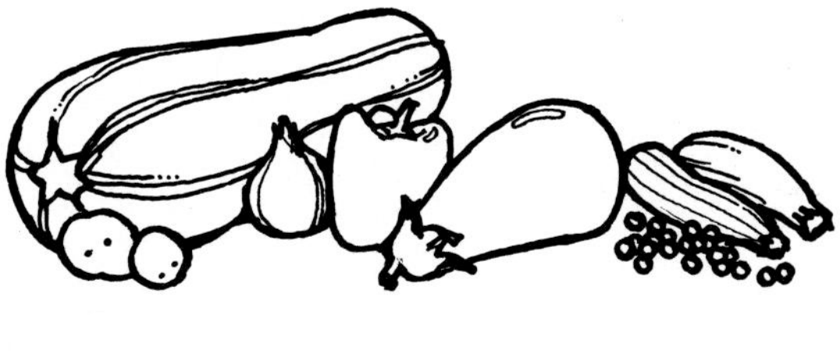

Sweet and Sour Duck with Pineapple ►

METRIC/IMPERIAL	AMERICAN
3 tablespoons soy sauce	*3 tablespoons soy sauce*
1 tablespoon sugar	*1 tablespoon sugar*
½ teaspoon ground ginger	*½ teaspoon ground ginger*
1 garlic clove, crushed	*1 garlic clove, crushed*
1¼ to 1¾ kg./4 lb. duck, cut into serving pieces	*4 lb. duck, cut into serving pieces*
500 ml./1 pint water	*2½ cups water*
1 small onion, roughly chopped	*1 small onion, roughly chopped*
1 small bay leaf	*1 small bay leaf*
1 bouquet garni	*1 bouquet garni*
salt and pepper	*salt and pepper*
2 tablespoons oil	*2 tablespoons oil*
400 g./14 oz. can pineapple chunks	*14 oz. can pineapple chunks*
1 tablespoon cornflour	*1 tablespoon cornstarch*
2 tablespoons vinegar	*2 tablespoons vinegar*

Blend together the soy sauce, sugar, ginger and garlic. Add the duck pieces and leave to marinate for 1 hour. Put the duck giblets into a pan with the water, onion, bay leaf, bouquet garni and seasoning. Bring slowly to the boil, remove any scum from the surface, then cover the pan and simmer gently for 1 hour. Strain and reserve the stock.

Heat the oil in a large flameproof casserole. Add the duck pieces and fry on all sides until golden brown. Make the duck stock up to 625 ml./1¼ pints (3 cups) with the syrup from the can of pineapple and extra water if necessary. Pour over the duck, together with any remaining marinade. Cover and cook in a moderate oven, 180°C, 350°F, Gas Mark 4 for 1 hour.

Blend the cornflour (cornstarch) with the vinegar in a saucepan, then drain the liquid from the casserole into the pan. Bring to the boil on top of the stove, stirring all the time. Add the pineapple chunks, taste and adjust the seasoning, then pour back over the duck. Replace in the oven and cook uncovered for a further 10 minutes. **Serves 4**

Duck with Turnips

METRIC/IMPERIAL	AMERICAN
1¾ kg./4 lb. duck	*4 lb. duck*
salt and pepper	*salt and pepper*
25 g./1 oz. butter	*2 tablespoons butter*
400 g./1 lb. young turnips, quartered	*1 lb. young turnips, quartered*
1 tablespoon sugar	*1 tablespoon sugar*
750 ml./1½ pints stock	*3¾ cups stock*
1 bouquet garni	*1 bouquet garni*
1 large onion, quartered	*1 large onion, quartered*
1 tablespoon flour	*1 tablespoon flour*

Season the duck inside and out with salt and pepper. Melt the butter in a large flameproof casserole. Add the duck and cook on all sides until it is golden brown. Remove from the casserole and put on one side. Add the turnips to the casserole with the sugar and cook for 10 minutes or until golden. Pour in the stock, add the bouquet garni and onion and return the duck to the casserole. Cover and cook in a moderate oven, 180°C, 350°F, Gas Mark 4 for 1 hour. Remove the lid of the casserole and cook for a further 30 minutes to crisp the skin of the duck.

Remove the duck and turnips from the casserole and arrange on a serving dish. Skim all the excess fat off the duck stock and remove the bouquet garni and onion. Put the casserole over high heat and boil the stock rapidly until it is reduced by half. Blend the flour with 1 tablespoon of the duck fat and add to the stock a teaspoon at a time, stirring well. Serve this sauce separately with the duck. **Serves 4**

French Rabbit Stew

METRIC/IMPERIAL	AMERICAN
4 to 6 rabbit pieces	*4 to 6 rabbit pieces*
salt and pepper	*salt and pepper*
15 g./½ oz. butter	*1 tablespoon butter*
1 garlic clove, crushed	*1 garlic clove, crushed*
4 streaky bacon rashers, chopped	*4 fatty bacon slices, chopped*
400 g./1 lb. button onions	*1 lb. button onions*
25 g./1 oz. flour	*¼ cup flour*
125 ml./¼ pint water	*⅝ cup water*
125 ml./¼ pint red wine	*⅝ cup red wine*
100 g./4 oz. mushrooms	*4 oz. mushrooms*
2 bay leaves	*2 bay leaves*

Wash the rabbit pieces well and dry them. Season each with salt and pepper. Melt the butter in a pan and fry the garlic, bacon and onions until golden brown. Remove from the pan with a slotted spoon and place in a casserole. Add the rabbit pieces to the pan and fry these for 5 minutes or until browned on all sides. Remove from the pan and put into the casserole. Stir the flour into the fat remaining in the pan and cook over a very gentle heat for about 10 minutes, stirring from time to time, until it becomes a rich brown colour. Gradually stir in the water and wine and bring to the boil, stirring all the time. Pour over the rabbit in the casserole and add the mushrooms and bay leaves. Cover the casserole and cook in a moderate oven, 180°C, 350°F, Gas Mark 4 for 1½ hours. Taste and adjust the seasoning before serving. **Serves 4 to 6**

Casseroled Guinea Fowl with Celery

METRIC/IMPERIAL	AMERICAN
1 tablespoon olive oil	*1 tablespoon olive oil*
25 g./1 oz. butter	*2 tablespoons butter*
2 guinea fowl	*2 guinea fowl*
3 heads of celery	*3 heads of celery*
125 ml./¼ pint dry white wine	*⅝ cup dry white wine*
125 ml./¼ pint water	*⅝ cup water*
salt and pepper	*salt and pepper*
125 ml./¼ pint double cream	*⅝ cup heavy cream*

Heat the oil and butter in a large pan and quickly fry the guinea fowl until they are golden brown all over. Remove them from the pan and place in a casserole. Scrub the celery, trim off the leaves and cut in half lengthways. Add the celery to the pan and fry quickly until golden brown, then add to the casserole. Add the wine and water to the pan, season with salt and pepper and bring to the boil. Pour into the casserole, cover and cook in a warm oven, 170°C, 325°F, Gas Mark 3 for 2 hours.

Remove the birds from the casserole and place on a serving dish surrounded by the celery. Boil the cooking liquid rapidly in an open pan until it is reduced to a scant 250 ml. /½ pint (1¼ cups), then add the cream and heat gently without boiling. Serve this sauce with the guinea fowl. **Serves 6**

Note: *If wishing to deep freeze this dish do not reduce the sauce and add the cream. Reheat gently, then boil the cooking liquid rapidly and continue as above.*

Hare in Madeira Sauce

METRIC/IMPERIAL
1 hare, cut into serving pieces
50 g./2 oz. flour
salt and pepper
1 teaspoon chopped fresh sage
4 tablespoons oil
4 streaky bacon rashers, chopped
250 ml./½ pint Madeira wine
125 ml./¼ pint stock
200 g./8 oz. button mushrooms
1 tablespoon chopped parsley

AMERICAN
1 hare, cut into serving pieces
½ cup flour
salt and pepper
1 teaspoon chopped fresh sage
4 tablespoons oil
4 fatty bacon slices, chopped
1¼ cups Madeira wine
⅝ cup stock
8 oz. button mushrooms
1 tablespoon chopped parsley

Coat the hare with the flour, seasoned with salt and pepper and the sage. Heat the oil in a large frying pan and fry the bacon and hare until it is golden brown on all sides. Remove from the pan and place in a casserole. Sprinkle in any remaining flour and cook for 1 minute, then add the Madeira and stock. Bring to the boil, stirring all the time. Pour over the hare in the casserole, cover and cook in a warm oven, 170°C, 325°F, Gas Mark 3 for 1½ hours. Add the mushrooms to the casserole and continue cooking for 30 minutes. Serve sprinkled with parsley.

Serves 6 to 8

Casseroled Pheasant or Grouse

METRIC/IMPERIAL	AMERICAN
1 large pheasant or 2 grouse	*1 large pheasant or 2 grouse*
25 g./1 oz. butter	*2 tablespoons butter*
1 tablespoon oil	*1 tablespoon oil*
1 large onion, sliced	*1 large onion, sliced*
50 g./2 oz. flour	*½ cup flour*
500 ml./1 pint stock	*2½ cups stock*
finely grated rind and juice of 1 orange	*finely grated rind and juice of 1 orange*
1 tablespoon redcurrant jelly	*1 tablespoon redcurrant jelly*
125 ml./¼ pint port wine	*⅝ cup port wine*
1 bay leaf	*1 bay leaf*
1 parsley sprig	*1 parsley sprig*
salt and pepper	*salt and pepper*

Cut the pheasant into four or cut each grouse in half. Heat the butter and oil in a pan and quickly fry the birds on all sides until a good golden colour. Remove from the pan and place in a casserole. Add the onion to the pan and cook until soft. Stir in the flour and cook, stirring, for about 5 minutes, or until golden brown. Gradually add the stock and bring to the boil, stirring all the time. Allow to thicken and add the remaining ingredients. Pour over the pheasant or grouse in the casserole, cover and cook in a warm oven, 170°C, 325°F, Gas Mark 3 for 2 to 4 hours depending on the age of the birds. Taste and adjust the seasoning before serving. **Serves 4**

Pigeons with Redcurrant Jelly

METRIC/IMPERIAL	AMERICAN
2 tablespoons oil	*2 tablespoons oil*
8 back bacon rashers	*8 lean bacon slices*
1 onion, finely chopped	*1 onion, finely chopped*
4 wood pigeons	*4 wood pigeons*
4 tablespoons redcurrant jelly	*4 tablespoons redcurrant jelly*
250 ml./½ pint stock	*1¼ cups stock*
½ teaspoon grated nutmeg	*½ teaspoon grated nutmeg*
salt and pepper	*salt and pepper*
200 g./8 oz. green grapes	*8 oz. green grapes*

Heat the oil in a frying pan. Roughly chop half the bacon and add to the pan with the onion. Fry for about 5 minutes. Remove from the pan with a slotted spoon and place in a casserole. Lay a rasher (slice) of bacon over the breast of each pigeon, add the pigeons to the pan and fry on all sides until browned. Add to the casserole. Put the jelly, stock, nutmeg and seasoning into the frying pan and bring just to the boil. Pour over the pigeons in the casserole. Cover and cook in a warm oven, 170°C, 325°F, Gas Mark 3 for 3 hours. Add the grapes and cook for a further 5 minutes. **Serves 4**

Hunters' Casserole

METRIC/IMPERIAL	AMERICAN
2 tablespoons oil	*2 tablespoons oil*
200 g./8 oz. streaky bacon, chopped	*8 oz. fatty bacon, chopped*
4 onions, chopped	*4 onions, chopped*
2 carrots, quartered	*2 carrots, quartered*
600 g./1½ lb. venison or 1 kg./2½ lb. rabbit or hare	*1½ lb. venison or 2½ lb. rabbit or hare*
40 g./1½ oz. flour	*6 tablespoons flour*
salt and pepper	*salt and pepper*
250 ml./½ pint red wine	*1¼ cups red wine*
425 g./15 oz. can tomatoes	*15 oz. can tomatoes*
1 bay leaf	*1 bay leaf*
chopped parsley	*chopped parsley*

Heat the oil in a large pan and fry the bacon, onions and carrots for 10 minutes. Remove from the pan and place in a casserole. Cut the venison into 2½ cm./1 in. cubes, or joint the rabbit or hare. Coat with the flour, seasoned with salt and pepper, and fry in the fat remaining in the pan until brown on all sides. Remove from the pan and add to the vegetables in the casserole. Add the wine, tomatoes, with the juice from the can, and bay leaf to the frying pan. Bring to the boil and pour into the casserole. Cover and cook in a warm oven, 170°C, 325°F, Gas Mark 3 for 2½ hours. Remove the bay leaf, garnish with parsley and serve with boiled rice. **Serves 6**

Hare with Prunes

METRIC/IMPERIAL
150 g./6 oz. prunes
250 ml./½ pint red wine
1 hare, with the liver, cut into serving pieces
4 tablespoons water
40 g./1½ oz. flour
salt and pepper
75 g./3 oz. dripping
3 onions, chopped
2 garlic cloves, crushed (optional)
500 ml./1 pint brown stock
juice of ½ lemon
2 tablespoons redcurrant jelly
1 bouquet garni
2 to 3 slices white bread
25 g./1 oz. butter

AMERICAN
2 cups prunes
1¼ cups red wine
1 hare, with the liver, cut into serving pieces
4 tablespoons water
6 tablespoons flour
salt and pepper
⅜ cup dripping
3 onions, chopped
2 garlic cloves, crushed (optional)
2½ cups brown stock
juice of ½ lemon
2 tablespoons redcurrant jelly
1 bouquet garni
2 to 3 slices white bread
2 tablespoons butter

Soak the prunes in the red wine overnight. Put the hare liver into a saucepan with the water and simmer gently for 20 minutes or until tender. Mash with the cooking liquid. Coat the hare with the flour, seasoned with salt and pepper.

Heat the dripping in a large flameproof casserole and fry the hare quickly on all sides until golden. Remove from the casserole and put on one side. Fry the onions and garlic, if using, in the fat remaining in the casserole for about 5 minutes or until soft. Stir in any remaining flour, then gradually stir in the stock. Bring slowly to the boil, stirring all the time. Add the lemon juice, mashed liver mixture, redcurrant jelly, prunes, with the wine, and bouquet garni. Season well. Replace the hare in the casserole, cover and cook in a warm oven, 170°C, 325°F, Gas Mark 3 for 3 hours.

Remove the crusts from the bread and cut into triangles. Melt the butter in a frying pan and fry the bread until golden brown on both sides. Taste the hare casserole, adjust the seasoning and remove the bouquet garni. Turn into one large or six to eight smaller serving dishes and garnish with the croûtes. **Serves 6 to 8**

Fish Casseroles

People often choose fish because it can be cooked very quickly, by frying or grilling (broiling), and, unlike meat, you do not have to pay more for quick-cooking cuts. However, fish that is cooked in the oven is generally very moist and full of flavour, so it is well worth trying a fish casserole. Deep freeze owners will find this chapter especially useful as halfway through using large packs of fish steaks or fillets you may run out of different ideas of how to cook them. Once the casserole has been cooked it is also possible to re-freeze it, although I personally do not feel that a fish casserole freezes quite as well as many of the meat casseroles.

Smoked Cod with Corn

METRIC/IMPERIAL
25 g./1 oz. butter
1 small onion, chopped
1 green pepper, seeded and chopped
2 tablespoons chopped parsley
326 g./12 oz. can sweetcorn kernels, drained
400 to 600 g./1 to 1¼ lb. smoked cod fillet
freshly ground black pepper
125 ml./¼ pint single cream

AMERICAN
2 tablespoons butter
1 small onion, chopped
1 green pepper, seeded and chopped
2 tablespoons chopped parsley
12 oz. can sweetcorn kernels, drained
1 to 1¼ lb. smoked cod fillet
freshly ground black pepper
⅝ cup light cream

Melt the butter in a small pan, add the onion and green pepper and fry for about 8 minutes. Add the parsley and sweetcorn, mix together and turn into a casserole. Cut the cod into four to eight pieces and place on top of the vegetables in the casserole. Season with pepper and pour over the cream. Cover and cook in a moderate oven, 180°C, 350°F, Gas Mark 4 for 30 to 35 minutes. **Serves 4**

Note: *Do not deep freeze the cooked dish.*

Casseroled Herrings, Country Style

METRIC/IMPERIAL
25 g./1 oz. butter
2 large onions, thinly sliced
100 g./4 oz. streaky bacon, chopped
600 g./1½ lb. potatoes, thinly sliced
salt and pepper
125 ml./¼ pint milk
4 herrings, cleaned and boned
2 teaspoons French mustard

AMERICAN
2 tablespoons butter
2 large onions, thinly sliced
4 oz. fatty bacon, chopped
1½ lb. potatoes, thinly sliced
salt and pepper
⅝ cup milk
4 herrings, cleaned and boned
2 teaspoons French mustard

Melt the butter in a small pan and fry the onions gently for 5 minutes. Add the bacon and fry for a further 5 minutes. Place a third of the potatoes in a greased, ovenproof dish. Cover with half the onion and bacon mixture. Season each layer with salt and pepper. Repeat layers once and finally cover with a layer of potato. Pour over the milk. Cover and bake in a moderately hot oven, 190°C, 375°F, Gas Mark 5 for 1 hour.

Spread the herrings with the mustard and roll up from the head end. Remove the lid from the dish and place the herrings on top of the potatoes. Cover and return to the oven to cook for a further 25 minutes. **Serves 4**

Fish Poached in White Wine

One of the nicest and simplest ways of cooking fish is to poach it in liquid in the oven as this keeps it very moist. Serve hot with Hollandaise sauce, or cold with French dressing or mayonnaise.

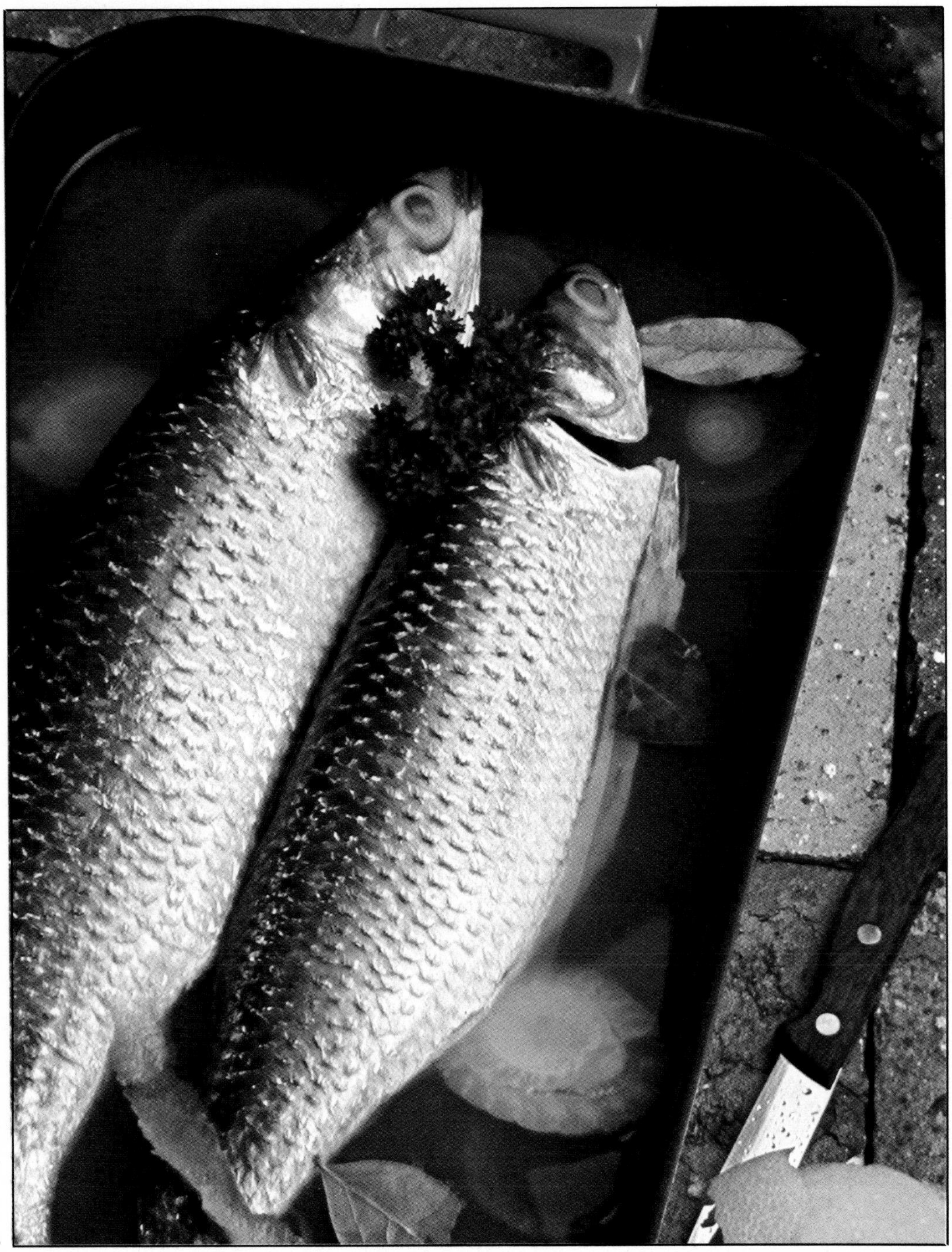

METRIC/IMPERIAL
2 large or 4 small mackerel, herring or grey mullet
250 ml./½ pint dry white wine or cider
375 ml./¾ pint water
1 onion, sliced
few fennel sprigs
finely pared rind of ½ lemon
4 peppercorns
1 bay leaf
salt

AMERICAN
2 large or 4 small mackerel, herring or grey mullet
1¼ cups dry white wine or cider
2 cups water
1 onion, sliced
few fennel sprigs
finely pared rind of ½ lemon
4 peppercorns
1 bay leaf
salt

Clean the fish and place in a casserole. Put the wine or cider, water, onion, fennel, lemon rind, peppercorns, bay leaf and salt into a pan and simmer gently for 10 minutes. Pour over the fish in the casserole. Cover and cook in a moderate oven, 180°C, 350°F, Gas Mark 4 for 40 minutes or until the fish is cooked. Serve either hot or cold (see above). **Serves 4**

Note: *Do not deep freeze the cooked dish.*

Piquant Fish Casserole

METRIC/IMPERIAL
2 teaspoons French mustard
4 large or 8 small plaice fillets
salt and pepper
25 g./1 oz. butter
150 g./6 oz. mushrooms, sliced
1 tablespoon chopped chives or spring onions
1 tablespoon chopped parsley
125 ml./¼ pint single cream

AMERICAN
2 teaspoons French mustard
4 large or 8 small flounder fillets
salt and pepper
2 tablespoons butter
6 oz. mushrooms, sliced
1 tablespoon chopped chives or scallions
1 tablespoon chopped parsley
⅝ cup light cream

Spread a little of the mustard on one side of each fish fillet and season with salt and pepper. Roll the fillets up, starting at the head and keeping the mustard inside, and place in a shallow casserole.

Melt the butter in a small pan and fry the mushrooms for 2 minutes. Add the chives or spring onions (scallions), parsley, cream and a little seasoning and pour over the fish. Cover and cook in a moderate oven, 180°C, 350°F, Gas Mark 4 for 20 to 30 minutes or until the fish is cooked. **Serves 4**

Note: *Do not freeze the cooked dish.*

Sole with Shrimps

METRIC/IMPERIAL
200 g./8 oz. potted shrimps
4 large or 8 small fillets of sole
salt and freshly ground black pepper
2 tablespoons chopped fresh dill or fennel
500 ml./1 pint single cream

AMERICAN
8 oz. potted shrimps
4 large or 8 small fillets of sole
salt and freshly ground black pepper
2 tablespoons chopped fresh dill or fennel
2½ cups light cream

Cook the shrimps in a saucepan over a very gentle heat until the butter has melted. Strain the butter into a shallow casserole and brush all over the sides. Season the fillets of sole with salt and pepper and divide the shrimps and half the chopped dill or fennel between them. Roll up the fillets and place in the casserole. Pour over the cream and season with more salt and pepper. Cover and cook in a moderately hot oven, 190°C, 375°F, Gas Mark 5 for 20 to 25 minutes or until the fish is cooked. Serve sprinkled with the remaining chopped dill or fennel. **Serves 4**

Fish with Grapes and Peppers

This particular recipe is a very easy one for slimmers.

METRIC/IMPERIAL
4 to 6 small plaice or whiting fillets
salt and pepper
125 ml./¼ pint dry cider, white wine or fish stock
1 small green pepper, seeded and chopped
1 small red pepper, seeded and chopped
50 g./2 oz. green grapes, halved and pipped

AMERICAN
4 to 6 small flounder or whiting fillets
salt and pepper
⅝ cup dry cider, white wine or fish stock
1 small green pepper, seeded and chopped
1 small red pepper, seeded and chopped
⅓ cup halved and seeded green grapes

Season the fish fillets, fold in half and place in an ovenproof dish. Pour over the cider, white wine or fish stock and add the green and red peppers and grapes. Cover and cook in a moderate oven, 180°C, 350°F, Gas Mark 4 for 20 to 30 minutes or until the fish is cooked. **Serves 4**

Note: *Do not freeze this dish.*

Herrings à la Greque

METRIC/IMPERIAL
4 herrings, cleaned and boned
3 tablespoons olive oil
1 onion, grated
1 garlic clove, crushed
1 tablespoon tomato purée
2 teaspoons lemon juice
salt and pepper
100 g./4 oz. button mushrooms, sliced
1 tablespoon chopped parsley

AMERICAN
4 herrings, cleaned and boned
3 tablespoons olive oil
1 onion, grated
1 garlic clove, crushed
1 tablespoon tomato purée
2 teaspoons lemon juice
salt and pepper
4 oz. button mushrooms, sliced
1 tablespoon chopped parsley

Place the herrings in a shallow casserole. Blend the oil, onion, garlic, tomato purée, lemon juice and seasoning together. Add the mushrooms and pour over the herrings. Cover and cook in a moderate oven, 180°C, 350°F, Gas Mark 4 for 30 to 35 minutes or until the herrings are cooked. Serve sprinkled with chopped parsley. **Serves 4**

Trout with White Wine

METRIC/IMPERIAL
4 trout
salt and pepper
50 g./2 oz. butter
1 small onion, very finely chopped
200 g./8 oz. button mushrooms, finely chopped
2 tablespoons chopped parsley
1 tablespoon lemon juice
125 ml./¼ pint dry white wine

AMERICAN
4 trout
salt and pepper
¼ cup butter
1 small onion, very finely chopped
8 oz. button mushrooms, finely chopped
2 tablespoons chopped parsley
1 tablespoon lemon juice
⅝ cup dry white wine

Clean the trout and season inside and out with salt and pepper. Melt the butter in a small pan and fry the onion gently for 5 minutes. Add the mushrooms and cook for a further 2 to 3 minutes, then add the parsley and lemon juice. Use this mixture to stuff the cavity in each fish and place in an ovenproof dish. Pour over the wine, cover and cook in a moderately hot oven, 190°C, 375°F, Gas Mark 5 for 30 minutes. **Serves 4**

Psari Plaki

METRIC/IMPERIAL
4 small herrings, mackerel or grey mullet
salt and pepper
juice of ½ lemon
5 tablespoons oil
2 onions, sliced
400 g./1 lb. potatoes, sliced
2 carrots, sliced
2 celery stalks, chopped
200 g./8 oz. tomatoes, peeled and sliced
1 tablespoon chopped parsley

AMERICAN
4 small herrings, mackerel or grey mullet
salt and pepper
juice of ½ lemon
5 tablespoons oil
2 onions, sliced
1 lb. potatoes, sliced
2 carrots, sliced
2 celery stalks, chopped
8 oz. tomatoes, peeled and sliced
1 tablespoon chopped parsley

Clean the fish, season with salt and pepper and place in an ovenproof dish. Sprinkle with the lemon juice. Heat the oil in a frying pan and fry the vegetables separately, first the onions, then the potatoes, carrots, celery and tomatoes. Arrange the vegetables around the fish. Cover and cook in a moderate oven, 180°C, 350°F, Gas Mark 4 for 1 hour. Sprinkle with parsley before serving. **Serves 4**

Provençale Fish Casserole

METRIC/IMPERIAL
1 medium-sized aubergine, cubed
3 courgettes, thinly sliced
salt and freshly ground black pepper
4 tablespoons olive oil
1 red pepper, seeded and chopped
2 garlic cloves, crushed
400 g./1 lb. tomatoes, peeled, seeded and quartered
2 tablespoons chopped parsley
4 cod steaks

AMERICAN
1 medium-sized eggplant, cubed
3 zucchini, thinly sliced
salt and freshly ground black pepper
4 tablespoons olive oil
1 red pepper, seeded and chopped
2 garlic cloves, crushed
1 lb. tomatoes, peeled, seeded and quartered
2 tablespoons chopped parsley
4 cod steaks

Put the aubergine (eggplant) cubes into a strainer with the courgettes (zucchini) and sprinkle with a teaspoon of salt. Leave to drain for 30 minutes. Heat the oil in a pan and fry the aubergine (eggplant), courgettes (zucchini), red pepper and garlic for about 8 minutes, then add the tomatoes, parsley and pepper. Cover and simmer for 30 minutes. Lay the cod steaks in a casserole and season with salt and pepper. Spoon the vegetable mixture over the fish, cover and bake in a moderate oven, 180°C, 350°F, Gas Mark 4 for 35 minutes. **Serves 4**

Mackerel with Tomatoes and Garlic

METRIC/IMPERIAL
4 medium-sized fresh mackerel, cleaned
salt and pepper
2 tablespoons olive oil
600 g./1½ lb. tomatoes, peeled, seeded and quartered
25 g./1 oz. butter
3 tablespoons fresh white breadcrumbs
1 tablespoon chopped parsley
1 garlic clove, crushed

AMERICAN
4 medium-sized fresh mackerel, cleaned
salt and pepper
2 tablespoons olive oil
1½ lb. tomatoes, peeled, seeded and quartered
2 tablespoons butter
3 tablespoons fresh white breadcrumbs
1 tablespoon chopped parsley
1 garlic clove, crushed

Season the mackerel with salt and pepper, inside and out. Heat the oil in a large frying pan and quickly fry the tomatoes for about 5 minutes, then place in a lightly greased casserole. Add the butter to the frying pan, leave it to melt, then fry the mackerel for 5 minutes on each side. Remove from the pan and place on top of the tomatoes in the casserole. Mix the breadcrumbs with the parsley and garlic and sprinkle over the fish. Spoon over the butter remaining from cooking the fish. Cook, uncovered, in a moderately hot oven, 200°C, 400°F, Gas Mark 6 for 25 minutes. **Serves 4**

Crispy-Topped Cod Casserole

METRIC/IMPERIAL
400 g./1 lb. skinned cod fillets
25 g./1 oz. butter
1 large onion, chopped
50 g./2 oz. button mushrooms sliced
200 g./8 oz. tomatoes, peeled and sliced
1 tablespoon chopped parsley
salt and pepper

For the topping:
6 slices white bread, crusts removed
25 g./1 oz. grated Cheddar cheese

AMERICAN
1 lb. skinned cod fillets
2 tablespoons butter
1 large onion, chopped
2 oz. button mushrooms, sliced
8 oz. tomatoes, peeled and sliced
1 tablespoon chopped parsley
salt and pepper

For the topping:
6 slices white bread, crusts removed
¼ cup grated Cheddar cheese

Lay the cod fillets in a buttered, shallow ovenproof dish. Melt the butter in a frying pan and fry the onion for 5 minutes. Add the mushrooms and fry for a further minute. Stir in the tomatoes and parsley and season well with salt and pepper. Spoon over the fish. Cover and cook in a moderate oven, 180°C, 350°F, Gas Mark 4 for 40 minutes.

Cut the slices of bread into triangles and lay them close together on a baking sheet. Sprinkle over the grated cheese and bake in the oven on the shelf below the fish. Arrange the triangles around the outside of the fish before serving. **Serves 4**

Herrings with Mushrooms

METRIC/IMPERIAL
4 herrings
1 large onion, very finely chopped
100 g./4 oz. mushrooms, finely chopped
3 tablespoons chopped parsley
1 tablespoon lemon juice
salt and pepper

To garnish:
few parsley sprigs
½ lemon, sliced

AMERICAN
4 herrings
1 large onion, very finely chopped
4 oz. mushrooms, finely chopped
3 tablespoons chopped parsley
1 tablespoon lemon juice
salt and pepper

To garnish:
few parsley sprigs
½ lemon, sliced

Clean the herrings and remove the heads. Mix the onion, mushrooms, parsley, lemon juice and seasoning together and use to stuff the herrings. Lay the stuffed herrings in a shallow casserole or deep ovenproof plate. Cover and cook in a moderate oven, 180°C, 350°F, Gas Mark 4 for 30 minutes. Garnish with parsley sprigs and lemon slices. **Serves 4**

Tuna Niçoise

METRIC/IMPERIAL
2 × 198 g./7 oz. cans tuna fish
juice of ½ lemon
salt and black pepper
4 anchovy fillets
1 tablespoon olive oil
1 onion, chopped
4 tomatoes, peeled, seeded and chopped
1 garlic clove, crushed
1 bouquet garni
125 ml./¼ pint white wine
2 tablespoons chopped parsley

AMERICAN
2 × 7 oz. cans tuna fish
juice of ½ lemon
salt and black pepper
4 anchovy fillets
1 tablespoon olive oil
1 onion, chopped
4 tomatoes, peeled, seeded and chopped
1 garlic clove, crushed
1 bouquet garni
⅝ cup white wine
2 tablespoons chopped parsley

Carefully remove the tuna from the cans, so that they stay in shape, and place side by side in an ovenproof dish. Sprinkle them with the lemon juice, season lightly with salt and pepper and arrange the anchovy fillets on the top.

Heat the oil in a small saucepan, add the onion and cook for 5 minutes. Add the tomatoes, garlic, bouquet garni and wine and boil rapidly in the open pan until reduced and thickened. Season to taste, remove the bouquet garni and pour over the tuna. Cover and cook in a moderate oven, 180°C, 350°F, Gas Mark 4 for 15 minutes. Serve sprinkled with the chopped parsley.

Serves 4

Cornish Casserole

A particularly good dish for those inevitable 'unexpected meals', this makes use of traditional storecupboard and frozen foods and only takes a short time to prepare.

METRIC/IMPERIAL
400 g./1 lb. leeks or onions, sliced
200 g./8 oz. potatoes, diced
50 g./2 oz. butter
396 g./14 oz. packet frozen cod steaks, diced
425 g./15 oz. can fish bisque
100 g./4 oz. frozen peas
salt and pepper

AMERICAN
1 lb. leeks or onions, sliced
8 oz. potatoes, diced
¼ cup butter
14 oz. package frozen cod steaks, diced
15 oz. can fish bisque
4 oz. frozen peas
salt and pepper

Fry the leeks or onions and potatoes in the butter in a frying pan for 10 minutes. Place in a casserole with the remaining ingredients. Cover and cook in a moderate oven, 180°C, 350°F, Gas Mark 4 for 1 hour.

Serves 4

Quick Tuna Casserole with Cheese Swirls

METRIC/IMPERIAL
2 × 198 g./7 oz. cans tuna fish
1 medium-sized onion, chopped
1 large green pepper, seeded and chopped
1 garlic clove, crushed
297 g./10½ oz. can condensed mushroom soup
125 ml./¼ pint milk
2 tablespoons lemon juice
1 tablespoon chopped parsley
1 tablespoon chopped chives
salt and pepper

For the cheese swirls:
200 g./8 oz. flour
2 teaspoons baking powder
¼ teaspoon salt
pinch of cayenne pepper
50 g./2 oz. butter or margarine
about 6 tablespoons milk
100 g./4 oz. Cheddar cheese, grated

AMERICAN
2 × 7 oz. cans tuna fish
1 medium-sized onion, chopped
1 large green pepper, seeded and chopped
1 garlic clove, crushed
10½ oz. can condensed mushroom soup
⅝ cup milk
2 tablespoons lemon juice
1 tablespoon chopped parsley
1 tablespoon chopped chives
salt and pepper

For the cheese swirls:
2 cups flour
2 teaspoons baking powder
½ teaspoon salt
pinch of cayenne pepper
¼ cup butter or margarine
about 6 tablespoons milk
1 cup grated Cheddar cheese

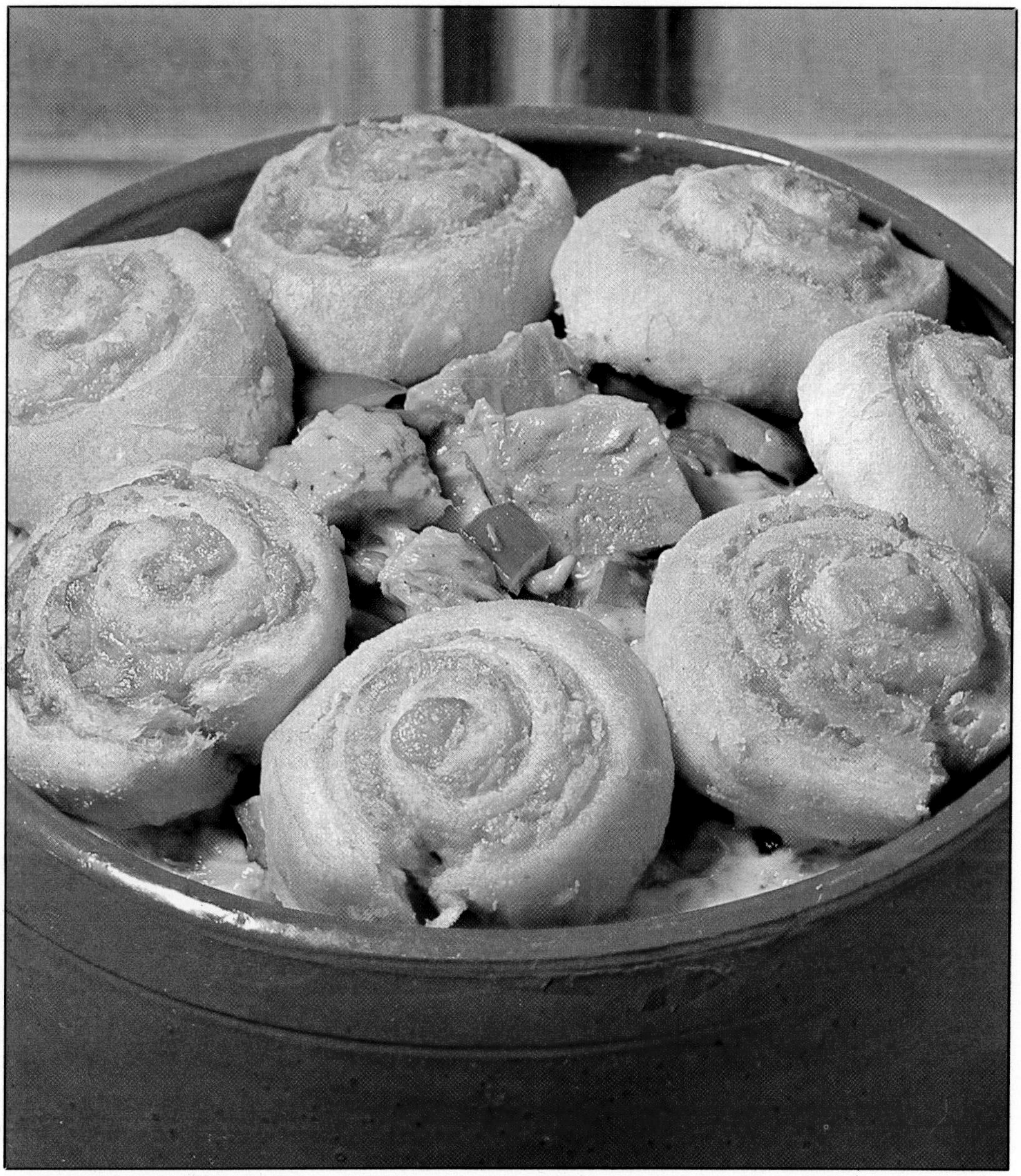

Drain off the oil from the tuna into a small saucepan. Fry the onion, green pepper and garlic in this for 5 minutes. Turn into a casserole with the tuna, soup, milk, lemon juice, herbs and seasoning and mix together. Cover and cook in a moderately hot oven, 200°C, 400°F, Gas Mark 6 for 30 minutes.

For the cheese swirls, sift the flour with the baking powder, salt and cayenne pepper. Rub in the butter or margarine until the mixture resembles fine breadcrumbs. Bind together with the milk to give a soft but not sticky dough. Roll out to a rectangle about ¾ cm./¼ in. thick. Sprinkle the surface with grated cheese and roll up like a Swiss (jelly) roll. Seal the edges and cut into slices about ¾ cm./¼ in. thick. Place on a baking sheet and bake above the casserole for 20 minutes. Top the tuna mixture with some of the cheese swirls before serving and serve the rest separately. **Serves 4**

Stuffed Fillets of Plaice (Flounder)

METRIC/IMPERIAL	AMERICAN
75 g./3 oz. butter	*$^3/_8$ cup butter*
2 shallots or small onions, finely chopped	*2 shallots or small onions, finely chopped*
50 g./2 oz. button mushrooms, finely chopped	*2 oz. button mushrooms, finely chopped*
50 g./2 oz. fresh white breadcrumbs	*1 cup fresh white breadcrumbs*
1 tablespoon chopped parsley	*1 tablespoon chopped parsley*
pinch of dried rosemary	*pinch of dried rosemary*
1 teaspoon grated lemon rind	*1 teaspoon grated lemon rind*
salt and pepper	*salt and pepper*
2 large plaice fillets	*2 large flounder fillets*
4 streaky bacon rashers	*4 fatty bacon slices*
600 g./ $1^1/_2$ lb. potatoes	*$1^1/_2$ lb. potatoes*
250 ml./$^1/_2$ pint milk	*$1^1/_4$ cups milk*

Melt two-thirds of the butter in a small pan and fry the shallots or onions and mushrooms for 5 minutes. Add the breadcrumbs and cook for a further 5 minutes until crisp, then add the parsley, rosemary, lemon rind and seasoning. Lay one fillet of plaice (flounder) in a large buttered, shallow casserole and season with salt and pepper. Spread the breadcrumb mixture all over it to within $1^1/_4$ cm./$^1/_2$ in. of the edge, then cover with the second fillet. Lightly season and top with the rashers (slices) of bacon.

Cook the potatoes in boiling salted water for 10 minutes. Drain and slice. Lay the potato slices all round the fish and pour the milk carefully over them. Cover the casserole and cook in a moderately hot oven, 190°C, 375°F, Gas Mark 5 for 30 minutes. Remove the lid, dot the potatoes with the remaining butter and cook for a further 15 minutes to crisp the bacon and potatoes. **Serves 4**

Cidered Haddock Casserole

METRIC/IMPERIAL	AMERICAN
400 g./1 lb. haddock or cod fillet	*1 lb. haddock or cod fillet*
200 g./8 oz. tomatoes, peeled and sliced	*8 oz. tomatoes, peeled and sliced*
50 g./2 oz. button mushrooms, sliced	*2 oz. button mushrooms, sliced*
1 onion, chopped	*1 onion, chopped*
1 tablespoon chopped parsley	*1 tablespoon chopped parsley*
salt and freshly ground black pepper	*salt and freshly ground black pepper*
5 tablespoons cider	*5 tablespoons cider*
2 tablespoons fresh white breadcrumbs	*2 tablespoons fresh white breadcrumbs*
2 tablespoons grated Cheddar cheese	*2 tablespoons grated Cheddar cheese*

Skin the fish and cut into cubes. Lay the fish cubes in a casserole, cover with the tomatoes, mushrooms and onion, then sprinkle with the parsley and seasoning. Pour over the cider, cover and cook in a moderate oven, 180°C, 350°F, Gas Mark 4 for 20 to 25 minutes or until the fish is cooked. Mix the breadcrumbs and cheese together. Sprinkle over the top of the fish, then put the dish under a hot grill (broiler) until the cheese and breadcrumbs are golden brown. **Serves 4**

Red Mullet (Snapper) Niçoise

METRIC/IMPERIAL	AMERICAN
For the stuffing:	For the stuffing:
1 tablespoon olive oil	*1 tablespoon olive oil*
1 small onion, finely chopped	*1 small onion, finely chopped*
1 small garlic clove, crushed	*1 small garlic clove, crushed*
50 g./2 oz. button mushrooms, finely chopped	*2 oz. button mushrooms, finely chopped*
2 tablespoons chopped parsley	*2 tablespoons chopped parsley*
salt and pepper	*salt and pepper*
For the fish:	For the fish:
4 red mullet, cleaned	*4 small red snapper, cleaned*
salt and pepper	*salt and pepper*
125 ml./$^1/_4$ pint dry white wine	*$^5/_8$ cup dry white wine*
few fennel sprigs	*few fennel sprigs*

Heat the oil in a small pan and fry the onion and garlic gently for 5 minutes. Add the mushrooms and cook for a further 2 to 3 minutes, then remove from the heat and add the parsley and seasoning.

Season the fish lightly with salt and pepper inside and out and put a tablespoonful of the stuffing into the stomach cavity of each. Lay the fish in a shallow casserole, pour over the wine and add the sprigs of fennel. Cover and bake in a moderately hot oven, 200°C, 400°F, Gas Mark 6 for 25 minutes or until the mullet (snapper) are cooked. **Serves 4**

Crab and Almonds with Rice

METRIC/IMPERIAL
200 g./8 oz. brown or white long-grain rice
500 ml./1 pint chicken stock, or water and 1 stock cube
2 tablespoons lemon juice
75 g./3 oz. butter
300 to 400 g./12 oz. to 1 lb. crabmeat, shell and cartilage removed
125 ml./¼ pint soured cream
salt and freshly ground black pepper
100 g./4 oz. blanched slivered almonds
2 tablespoons chopped parsley

To garnish:
few parsley sprigs
½ lemon, thinly sliced

AMERICAN
1⅓ cups brown or white long-grain rice
2½ cups chicken stock, or water and 1 stock cube
2 tablespoons lemon juice
⅜ cup butter
12 oz. to 1 lb. crabmeat, shell and cartilage removed
⅝ cup sour cream
salt and freshly ground black pepper
⅔ cup blanched slivered almonds
2 tablespoons chopped parsley

To garnish:
few parsley sprigs
½ lemon, thinly sliced

Put the rice, stock or water and stock cube and lemon juice in an ovenproof dish. Cover and cook in a moderate oven, 180°C, 350°F, Gas Mark 4 for 1¼ hours.

Melt two-thirds of the butter in a pan. Add the crabmeat and toss lightly, then stir in the soured cream and seasoning. Spoon over the rice, re-cover and cook for a further 15 minutes. Just before serving, quickly fry the almonds in the remaining butter until they are golden. Sprinkle over the top of the crabmeat and rice with the chopped parsley. Garnish with the parsley sprigs and sliced lemon. **Serves 4**

Note: *If you want to prepare this dish in advance, the rice can be cooked on top of the stove in a saucepan with the stock and lemon juice for 15 minutes. Turn into a casserole, prepare the crab as above, then re-heat in the oven for 30 minutes before serving. Do not freeze.*

Vegetable Casseroles

Vegetable casseroles fall into two categories: the vegetable side dish which you will serve with a main dish, and the composite vegetable casserole, such as Savoury Stuffed Marrow (Squash), which often forms a complete meal in one pot. These dishes are often fairly cheap as they tend to make the meat, usually the most expensive part of any main dish, 'go further' and the various stuffings given in this chapter can be interchanged or used with other vegetables according to personal taste. There are also very sustaining vegetarian dishes which usually contain peas or beans. The pulses, peas, beans, lentils, etc., have a high protein content and are an economical way of giving the family protein. They can either be used in conjunction with meat or they can provide the entire protein content of a meal.

The increasing cost of fuel has meant that it is more important than ever to use your oven to capacity, and if you are cooking a meat, poultry or game casserole it is also wise to cook the vegetables in the oven at the same time. Unfortunately many vegetables cannot be cooked in this way as they need to be put straight into boiling salted water to retain all their flavour and nutrients. Root vegetables, however, such as carrots and turnips, can be cooked very successfully in the oven and so can some of the more luxury vegetables such as aubergines (eggplants) and courgettes (zucchini). Potatoes baked in their jackets are one of the easiest vegetables of all, so I would recommend cooking potatoes in this way to serve with a casserole. Onions can also be cooked in their skins; this is an old French method from the days when people used to cook their food in the local baker's oven.

Lentils with Salt Pork

METRIC/IMPERIAL	AMERICAN
1 tablespoon oil	*1 tablespoon oil*
1 onion, chopped	*1 onion, chopped*
2 garlic cloves, crushed	*2 garlic cloves, crushed*
1 bouquet garni	*1 bouquet garni*
1 bay leaf	*1 bay leaf*
200 g./8 oz. brown or green lentils, soaked overnight and drained	*1⅓ cups brown or green lentils, soaked overnight and drained*
500 ml./1 pint water	*2½ cups water*
400 g./1 lb. salt pork, soaked overnight and drained	*1 lb. salt pork shoulder butt*
salt and freshly ground black pepper	*salt and freshly ground black pepper*

Heat the oil in a flameproof casserole, add the onion and garlic and fry gently for 5 minutes. Add the bouquet garni, bay leaf, lentils and water and bring to the boil. Add the piece of pork. Cover and cook in a cool oven, 150°C, 300°F, Gas Mark 2 for 2½ hours. Remove the bouquet garni and bay leaf. Taste and adjust the seasoning.

Serves 4

Aubergines (Eggplants) Provençale

METRIC/IMPERIAL	AMERICAN
2 large aubergines, thinly sliced	*2 large eggplants, thinly sliced*
1 tablespoon salt	*1 tablespoon salt*
olive oil	*olive oil*
1 large onion, sliced	*1 large onion, sliced*
1 garlic clove, crushed	*1 garlic clove, crushed*
200 g./8 oz. tomatoes, peeled and chopped	*8 oz. tomatoes, peeled and chopped*
1 tablespoon chopped parsley	*1 tablespoon chopped parsley*
freshly ground black pepper	*freshly ground black pepper*
25 g./1 oz. fresh white breadcrumbs	*½ cup fresh white breadcrumbs*

Put the aubergine (eggplant) slices into a colander, sprinkle with the salt and leave to drain for 30 minutes. Dry well with kitchen paper. Heat a little oil in a large frying pan and fry the aubergine (eggplant) slices, a few at a time, for 2 to 3 minutes on each side, then remove from the pan. Aubergines (eggplants) absorb a great deal of oil in frying, so fry them in the minimum amount of oil. When all the aubergines (eggplants) have been fried, heat 2 tablespoons of oil in the pan and gently fry the onion and garlic for 5 minutes. Add the tomatoes and parsley with plenty of pepper and cook for a further 5 minutes. Put half the aubergines (eggplants) in a casserole, spread over half the tomato mixture, then repeat these layers. Cover and cook in a moderately hot oven, 190°C, 375°F, Gas Mark 5 for 30 minutes. Remove the lid, sprinkle with the breadcrumbs and cook for a further 15 minutes uncovered. Serve hot or cold.

Serves 4 as a side dish

Chick Pea Casserole

This is an economical vegetarian casserole.

METRIC/IMPERIAL
200 g./8 oz. chick peas, soaked overnight and drained
salt and pepper
1 tablespoon oil
1 onion, chopped
1 garlic clove, crushed
400 g./1 lb. tomatoes, peeled and sliced
200 g./8 oz. cabbage, shredded
1 green pepper, seeded and chopped
½ teaspoon ground ginger
pinch of ground cloves

AMERICAN
1⅓ cups chick peas (garbanzos), soaked overnight and drained
salt and pepper
1 tablespoon oil
1 onion, chopped
1 garlic clove, crushed
1 lb. tomatoes, peeled and sliced
8 oz. cabbage, shredded
1 green pepper, seeded and chopped
½ teaspoon ground ginger
pinch of ground cloves

Put the chick peas in a pan with enough fresh cold water to cover and a little salt. Cover and simmer gently for about 2 hours or until tender.

Heat the oil in a large pan and fry the onion, garlic, tomatoes, cabbage and green pepper for about 10 minutes. Turn into a casserole and add the ginger, cloves and seasoning. Drain the chick peas and reserve the liquid. Add the peas to the vegetables, together with 250 ml./½ pint (1¼ cups) of the pea liquid. Cover and cook in a moderate oven, 180°C, 350°F, Gas Mark 4 for 1 hour. **Serves 4 to 6**

Rice and Bean Casserole

METRIC/IMPERIAL
1 onion, chopped
2 garlic cloves, crushed
1 green pepper, seeded and chopped
3 tablespoons oil
400 g./1 lb. long grain rice
3 carrots, diced
200 g./8 oz. green beans, fresh or frozen, chopped
400 g./14 oz. can kidney beans, drained
1 tablespoon chopped parsley
2 teaspoons salt
pepper
pinch of powdered saffron
¼ teaspoon ground turmeric
¼ teaspoon ground coriander
1 tablespoon yeast extract
1 l./2 pints water

AMERICAN
1 onion, chopped
2 garlic cloves, crushed
1 green pepper, seeded and chopped
3 tablespoons oil
2⅔ cups long grain rice
3 carrots, diced
8 oz. green beans, fresh or frozen, chopped
14 oz. can kidney beans, drained
1 tablespoon chopped parsley
2 teaspoons salt
pepper
pinch of powdered saffron
¼ teaspoon ground turmeric
¼ teaspoon ground coriander
1 tablespoon yeast extract
5 cups water

Fry the onion, garlic and green pepper in the oil in a small pan for 5 minutes. Put into a large casserole with the rice, all the vegetables and the parsley. Blend the salt, pepper, saffron, turmeric, coriander and yeast extract with the water. Pour over the vegetables in the casserole and mix well. Cover and cook in a moderate oven, 180°C, 350°F, Gas Mark 4 for 1¼ hours.
Serves 6

Courgettes (Zucchini) with Tomatoes

METRIC/IMPERIAL
400 g./1 lb. courgettes, sliced
salt and pepper
4 tablespoons olive oil
juice of ½ lemon
125 ml./¼ pint water
1 bay leaf
1 thyme sprig
4 coriander seeds, crushed
1 garlic clove, crushed
4 large tomatoes, peeled

AMERICAN
1 lb. zucchini, sliced
salt and pepper
4 tablespoons olive oil
juice of ½ lemon
⅝ cup water
1 bay leaf
1 thyme sprig
4 coriander seeds, crushed
1 garlic clove, crushed
4 large tomatoes, peeled

Put the courgettes (zucchini) slices into a colander, sprinkle with salt and leave to drain for 30 minutes. Put into a casserole with all the remaining ingredients, cover and cook in a moderate oven, 180°C, 350°F, Gas Mark 4 for 1 hour. Taste and adjust the seasoning and either serve hot or allow to cool and serve chilled. **Serves 4 as a side dish**

Savoury Stuffed Cabbage

METRIC/IMPERIAL
For the stuffing:
400 g./1 lb. salt pork belly
25 g./1 oz. butter
1 onion, chopped
2 celery stalks, finely chopped
2 garlic cloves, crushed
100 g./4 oz. crustless white bread
2 tablespoons chopped parsley
1 teaspoon chopped thyme
salt and pepper

For the cabbage:
1 large crisp cabbage, preferably a Savoy
salt
250 ml./½ pint well-flavoured stock
1 onion, chopped
2 carrots, chopped
2 leeks, chopped (optional)

AMERICAN
For the stuffing:
1 lb. salt pork fat back
2 tablespoons butter
1 onion, chopped
2 celery stalks, finely chopped
2 garlic cloves, crushed
4 oz. crustless white bread
2 tablespoons chopped parsley
1 teaspoon chopped thyme
salt and pepper

For the cabbage:
1 large crisp cabbage, preferably a Savoy
salt
1¼ cups well-flavoured stock
1 onion, chopped
2 carrots, chopped
2 leeks, chopped (optional)

Soak the salt pork for at least 4 hours or overnight in cold water. Drain, dry and remove all the skin and bone. Put through a fairly fine mincer (grinder) or food mill and turn into a bowl. Melt the butter in a small pan and fry the onion, celery and garlic for 5 minutes, then add to the pork. Soak the bread in cold water for 5 minutes, then wring completely dry in your hands. Add to the pork with the remaining stuffing ingredients and blend well.

Leave the cabbage whole, but remove about five of the large outside leaves. Cook both the whole cabbage and the leaves in boiling, salted water for 4 minutes. Drain and rinse in cold water. Very carefully open out the cabbage, leaf by leaf, and starting in the centre spread each leaf with a spoonful of the stuffing. Wrap the large leaves round the cabbage and tie the cabbage securely with string. Pour the stock into a large casserole and add the onion, carrots and leeks, if you are using them. Place the cabbage in the casserole, cover tightly and cook in a warm oven, 170°C, 325°F, Gas Mark 3 for 3 hours. Carefully take the cabbage out of the casserole and remove the string and large cabbage leaves. Arrange on a serving dish with the drained vegetables from the casserole and serve the stock separately. **Serves 6**

French Bean Pot with Sausages

METRIC/IMPERIAL
300 g./12 oz. haricot beans, soaked overnight and drained
400 g./1 lb. salt pork belly
1 large onion
3 cloves
1 bouquet garni
1 large garlic clove, crushed
400 g./1 lb. pork sausages
15 g./½ oz. bacon dripping or lard
70 g./2¼ oz. can tomato purée
1 teaspoon sugar
salt and pepper
4 tablespoons fresh white breadcrumbs (optional)

AMERICAN
2 cups haricot (dried white) beans, soaked overnight and drained
1 lb. salt pork fat back
1 large onion
3 cloves
1 bouquet garni
1 large garlic clove, crushed
1 lb. pork sausages
1 tablespoon bacon dripping or lard
2¼ oz. can tomato purée
1 teaspoon sugar
salt and pepper
4 tablespoons fresh white breadcrumbs (optional)

Put the beans into a large saucepan with the pork, the onion, peeled and studded with the cloves, the bouquet garni and the garlic. Cover with water and bring to the boil. Cover and simmer gently for 1½ hours or until the beans are tender.

Fry the sausages in the bacon dripping or lard until golden brown. Remove from the frying pan and cut each one into three or four pieces. Add the tomato purée to the pan with the sugar and stir over a very gentle heat for 2 to 3 minutes.

When the beans are cooked, lift out the pork and cut it into slices. Drain the beans, reserving the cooking liquid. Discard the bouquet garni and the cloves and chop the onion roughly. Put the beans into a casserole with the pork, onion and sausages. Blend 250 ml./½ pint (1¼ cups) of the reserved bean cooking liquid with the tomato purée mixture in the frying pan and bring to the boil. Season to taste and pour over the beans in the casserole. Mix well and, if necessary, add a little more cooking liquid so that the beans are moist, but not submerged. Sprinkle with the breadcrumbs and bake, uncovered if you want a crisp crust, or cover and bake in a moderate oven, 180°C, 350°F, Gas Mark 4 for 40 minutes. **Serves 4 to 6**

Spinach Niçoise

A rather unusual vegetable dish, this has the great advantage that it can be prepared in advance and given the final cooking in the oven just before you want to serve it.

METRIC/IMPERIAL
800 g./2 lb. spinach
salt and pepper
75 g./3 oz. butter
3 tablespoons double cream
pinch of grated nutmeg
2 onions, chopped
4 large tomatoes, peeled and chopped
100 g./4 oz. Cheddar, Gruyère or Emmenthal cheese, grated

AMERICAN
2 lb. spinach
salt and pepper
3/8 cup butter
3 tablespoons heavy cream
pinch of grated nutmeg
2 onions, chopped
4 large tomatoes, peeled and chopped
1 cup grated Cheddar, Gruyère or Emmenthal cheese

Wash the spinach well and remove the tough stalks. Bring to the boil 3/4 cm./1/4 in. water in a large saucepan with a teaspoon of salt. Add the spinach and cook for about 10 minutes or until it is quite tender. Drain well and chop finely. Return to the pan, stir in half the butter, all the cream, plenty of salt and pepper and the nutmeg. Put the spinach mixture into a casserole.

Melt the remaining butter in a small pan, add the onions and fry for 5 minutes. Add the tomatoes and cook gently for a further 5 minutes. Remove from the heat, stir in the grated cheese and spoon over the spinach. Cook, uncovered, in a moderately hot oven, 200°C, 400°F, Gas Mark 6 for 20 minutes or until the tomato mixture is a good golden colour.

Serves 4 to 6

Note: *Do not deep freeze this dish.*

Sweet and Sour Red Cabbage

METRIC/IMPERIAL
1 small red cabbage, shredded
2 cooking apples, peeled, cored and thinly sliced
2 medium-sized onions, thinly sliced
salt and freshly ground black pepper
2 tablespoons sugar
2 parsley sprigs
2 small bay leaves
¼ teaspoon dried thyme
2 tablespoons port
2 tablespoons wine vinegar
4 tablespooons soured cream (optional)

AMERICAN
1 small red cabbage, shredded
2 cooking apples, peeled, cored and thinly sliced
2 medium-sized onions, thinly sliced
salt and freshly ground black pepper
2 tablespoons sugar
2 parsley sprigs
2 small bay leaves
¼ teaspoon dried thyme
2 tablespoons port
2 tablespoons wine vinegar
4 tablespoons sour cream (optional)

Place the cabbage in a casserole in alternate layers with the apples and onions. Season each layer with salt, pepper and sugar. Put the herbs in the middle. Pour over the port and vinegar. Cover and cook in a cool oven, 150°C, 300°F, Gas Mark 2 for 2 hours. If wished, the soured cream can be stirred into the cabbage just before serving. **Serves 4 as a side dish**

Stuffed Peppers in Tomato Sauce

METRIC/IMPERIAL
4 green peppers
salt and pepper
2 tablespoons oil
1 onion, chopped
1 garlic clove, crushed
300 g./12 oz. minced pork
50 g./2 oz. fresh white breadcrumbs
1 egg, lightly beaten
¼ teaspoon grated nutmeg
pinch of dried sage

For the sauce;
1 tablespoon oil
4 streaky bacon rashers, chopped
1 onion, chopped
425 g./15 oz. can tomatoes
1 tablespoon tomato purée
½ teaspoon dried basil
salt and pepper

AMERICAN
4 green peppers
salt and pepper
2 tablespoons oil
1 onion, chopped
1 garlic clove, crushed
12 oz. ground pork
1 cup fresh white breadcrumbs
1 egg, lightly beaten
¼ teaspoon grated nutmeg
pinch of dried sage

For the sauce;
1 tablespoon oil
4 fatty bacon slices, chopped
1 onion, chopped
15 oz. can tomatoes
1 tablespoon tomato purée
½ teaspoon dried basil
salt and pepper

Cut the tops off the peppers and take out the core and seeds. Blanch the peppers, and the lids, in boiling salted water for 1 minute. Drain. Heat the oil in a small pan and fry the onion and garlic for 5 minutes. Remove from the heat, turn into a bowl and add the pork, breadcrumbs, egg, nutmeg and sage. Season well with salt and pepper. Blend together and divide between the four peppers. Top with their lids and place in a small, fairly deep casserole. If necessary cut a small slice off the base of each pepper so that they stand upright.

For the sauce, heat the oil in a pan and fry the bacon and onion for 5 minutes. Add the tomatoes, with the juice from the can, tomato purée, basil and seasoning. Bring to the boil and spoon round the peppers in the casserole. Cover and cook in a moderate oven, 180°C, 350°F, Gas Mark 4 for 1 hour.

Serves 4

Braised Chicory (Endive) with White Sauce

METRIC/IMPERIAL
600 g./1½ lb. chicory heads
25 g./1 oz. butter
¼ teaspoon grated nutmeg
juice of ½ lemon
125 ml./¼ pint chicken stock, or water and ¼ stock cube
1½ teaspoons cornflour
1 tablespoon water
2 tablespoons cream
salt and pepper
1½ tablespoons chopped parsley

AMERICAN
1½ lb. French or Belgian endive
2 tablespoons butter
¼ teaspoon grated nutmeg
juice of ½ lemon
⅝ cup chicken stock, or water and ¼ stock cube
1½ teaspoons cornstarch
1 tablespoon water
2 tablespoons cream
salt and pepper
1½ tablespoons chopped parsley

Wash and trim the chicory (endive), then plunge into boiling water for 1 minute. Drain and rinse in cold water. Drain again. Butter a large casserole and lay the chicory (endive) on the bottom in a single layer. Dot with butter. Stir the nutmeg and lemon juice into the stock, or water and stock cube, and pour over the chicory (endive) in the casserole. Cover and cook in a warm oven, 170°C, 325°F, Gas Mark 3 for 1½ hours.

Blend the cornflour (cornstarch) with the water. Drain the juices from the casserole into a small saucepan, add the cornflour (cornstarch) mixture and bring to the boil, stirring all the time. Allow to boil for 1 minute or until thickened. Remove from the heat, stir in the cream, season to taste and pour over the chicory (endive). Sprinkle with parsley.

Serves 4 as a side dish

Note: *If you do not want to serve the chicory (endive) with a white sauce you can omit this and just serve the vegetable in the casserole with the cooking liquid, sprinkled with parsley.*

Braised Celery

METRIC/IMPERIAL
4 small heads of celery
50 g./2 oz. butter
250 ml./½ pint stock
salt and pepper

AMERICAN
4 small heads of celery
¼ cup butter
1¼ cups stock
salt and pepper

Trim and scrub the celery heads, then tie securely with a piece of string to hold their shape. Melt the butter in a flameproof casserole and fry the celery until golden brown on all sides. Add the stock and seasoning. Cover and cook in a moderate oven, 180°C, 350°F, Gas Mark 4 for 1½ hours. Remove the string before serving.

Serves 4 as a side dish

Cauliflower Basket

This is a very good supper dish to prepare in advance and just heat through in the oven before serving. It is particularly good served with hot crusty granary bread which can be heated in the oven with the cauliflower for 5 minutes.

METRIC/IMPERIAL
1 medium-sized cauliflower
salt and pepper
25 g./1 oz. butter
25 g./1 oz. flour
125 ml./¼ pint milk
150 g./6 oz. Cheddar cheese, grated
2 hard-boiled eggs, chopped
1 tablespoon chopped gherkins
1 teaspoon capers
1 tablespoon chopped parsley
1 tablespoon chopped chives

AMERICAN
1 medium-sized cauliflower
salt and pepper
2 tablespoons butter
¼ cup flour
⅝ cup milk
1⅓ cups grated Cheddar cheese
2 hard-boiled eggs, chopped
1 tablespoon chopped gherkins
1 teaspoon capers
1 tablespoon chopped parsley
1 tablespoon chopped chives

Trim the cauliflower, but keep it whole. Cook in boiling salted water for 10 minutes, then drain and reserve the cooking liquid. Melt the butter in a pan, add the flour and cook for 1 minute. Gradually stir in the milk and 125 ml./¼ pint (⅝ cup) of the liquid from cooking the cauliflower. Bring to the boil, stirring all the time. Remove from the heat and stir in almost all the cheese, the eggs, gherkins, capers, parsley, chives and seasoning. Scoop out the centre part of the cauliflower, chop this coarsely and add to the sauce mixture.

Stand the cauliflower in a casserole, pile the cheese sauce mixture in the centre and top with the remainder of the cheese. Cook, uncovered, in a moderately hot oven, 200°C, 400°F, Gas Mark 6 for 30 minutes or until golden brown.

Serves 4

Aubergines (Eggplant) with Garlic

METRIC/IMPERIAL
4 medium-sized aubergines
2 garlic cloves, crushed
1 tablespoon chopped fresh marjoram
freshly ground black pepper
8 streaky bacon rashers
4 tablespoons olive oil

AMERICAN
4 medium-sized eggplants
2 garlic cloves, crushed
1 tablespoon chopped fresh marjoram
freshly ground black pepper
8 fatty bacon slices
4 tablespoons olive oil

Make two long slits in each aubergine (eggplant). Press a little crushed garlic, some marjoram and pepper into both sides of each bacon rasher (slice). Stuff a rasher (slice) of bacon into each slit and lay the aubergines (eggplants) in a shallow casserole. Pour over the oil, cover and cook in a warm oven, 170°C, 325°F, Gas Mark 3 for 1½ hours. Remove the lid and cook for a further 30 minutes uncovered. Serve hot or cold.
Serves 4

Savoury Stuffed Peppers

METRIC/IMPERIAL
4 large green peppers
salt
99 g./3½ oz. packet parsley and thyme stuffing
50 g./2 oz. mushrooms, finely chopped
1 medium-sized onion, finely chopped
300 g./12 oz. flaked corned beef or minced cooked beef or lamb
1 egg, lightly beaten
50 g./2 oz. butter, melted

AMERICAN
4 large green peppers
salt
3½ oz. envelope parsley and thyme stuffing
2 oz. mushrooms, finely chopped
1 medium-sized onion, finely chopped
12 oz. flaked corned beef or ground cooked beef or lamb
1 egg, lightly beaten
¼ cup butter, melted

Cut off the tops from the peppers and remove the cores and seeds. Put the peppers and the tops into a large pan of boiling, salted water and cook for 5 minutes. Drain well. Chop the tops of the peppers finely and put into a bowl with the parsley and thyme stuffing, mushrooms, onion and corned beef or cooked beef or lamb. Mix well and bind together with the egg and butter and water if necessary. Divide the mixture between the four peppers and place in a small, deep casserole. Cover tightly and cook in a moderate oven, 180°C, 350°F, Gas Mark 4 for 30 minutes.
Serves 4

Peas à la Français

METRIC/IMPERIAL
600 g./1½ lb. freshly shelled or frozen peas
1 lettuce heart, finely shredded
1 bunch spring onions, chopped
½ teaspoon salt
freshly ground black pepper
pinch of sugar
50 g./2 oz. butter, melted

AMERICAN
1½ lb. freshly shelled or frozen peas
1 lettuce heart, finely shredded
1 bunch scallions, chopped
½ teaspoon salt
freshly ground black pepper
pinch of sugar
¼ cup butter, melted

Put the peas, lettuce, spring onions (scallions), salt, pepper and sugar into a casserole. Pour over the butter and mix lightly. Cover and cook in a moderate oven, 180°C, 350°F, Gas Mark 4 for 1 hour.
Serves 6 as a side dish

Cucumbers in Cream

METRIC/IMPERIAL
1 large cucumber
salt and freshly ground black pepper
25 g./1 oz. butter
1 small bunch spring onions, chopped
½ teaspoon dried dill
4 tablespoons double cream

AMERICAN
1 large cucumber
salt and freshly ground black pepper
2 tablespooons butter
1 small bunch scallions, chopped
½ teaspoon dried dill
4 tablespoons heavy cream

Peel the cucumber, then cut into thin strips, about 2½ cm./1 in. long. Put into a colander, sprinkle with salt and leave for 30 minutes for the excess water to drain off. Put into a casserole with the butter, spring onions (scallions), dill and pepper. Cover and cook in a moderate oven, 180°C, 350°F, Gas Mark 4 for 45 minutes, stirring after about 5 minutes when the butter has melted. Stir in the cream, taste and adjust the seasoning and cook for a further 5 minutes.
Serves 4 as a side dish

Note: *Do not deep freeze this dish.*

Lentil and Vegetable Stew

METRIC/IMPERIAL
200 g./8 oz. orange lentils, soaked overnight and drained
1¼ l./2½ pints water
2 onions
2 cloves
1 bay leaf
4 garlic cloves
2 potatoes, coarsely chopped
3 medium-sized courgettes, coarsely chopped
2 leeks, trimmed and sliced
1 celery stalk, chopped
2 carrots, chopped
1 red pepper, seeded and chopped
salt and black pepper
1 tablespoon oil
3 tablespoons chopped parsley
juice of 2 lemons

AMERICAN
1⅓ cups orange lentils, soaked overnight and drained
6¼ cups water
2 onions
2 cloves
1 bay leaf
4 garlic cloves
2 potatoes, coarsely chopped
3 medium-sized zucchini, coarsely chopped
2 leeks, trimmed and sliced
1 celery stalk, chopped
2 carrots, chopped
1 red pepper, seeded and chopped
salt and black pepper
1 tablespoon oil
3 tablespoons chopped parsley
juice of 2 lemons

Put the lentils into a casserole with the water. Stick one of the onions with the cloves and put into the casserole with the bay leaf. Roughly chop two of the garlic cloves and add to the casserole. Cover and cook in a moderate oven, 180°C, 350°F, Gas Mark 4 for 1 hour. Remove the clove-stuck onion and add the potatoes, courgettes (zucchini), leeks, celery, carrots and red pepper. Season to taste, cover and cook for a further 1 hour.

Finely chop the remaining onion and crush the two remaining garlic cloves. Heat the oil in a frying pan and fry the onion and garlic for 5 minutes. Remove the casserole from the oven and add the onion and garlic, the parsley and lemon juice. Remove the bay leaf and taste and adjust the seasoning. Serve either hot or lightly chilled.

Serves 4 to 6

Vegetable Casserole

METRIC/IMPERIAL
2 tablespoons oil
2 large onions, coarsely chopped
2 garlic cloves, crushed
2 green peppers, seeded and chopped
400 g./1 lb. courgettes, sliced
2 medium-sized aubergines, sliced
200 g./8 oz. mushrooms
400 g./1 lb. tomatoes, peeled and sliced
70 g./2¼ oz. can tomato purée
2 bay leaves
1 tablespoon chopped parsley
1 teaspoon chopped fresh marjoram
1 teaspoon chopped fresh thyme
salt and pepper
250 ml./½ pint stock or water
2 large potatoes, peeled and thinly sliced
25 g./1 oz. butter

AMERICAN
2 tablespoons oil
2 large onions, coarsely chopped
2 garlic cloves, crushed
2 green peppers, seeded and chopped
1 lb. zucchini, sliced
2 medium-sized eggplants, sliced
8 oz. mushrooms
1 lb. tomatoes, peeled and sliced
2¼ oz. can tomato purée
2 bay leaves
1 tablespoon chopped parsley
1 teaspoon chopped fresh marjoram
1 teaspoon chopped fresh thyme
salt and pepper
1¼ cups stock or water
2 large potatoes, peeled and thinly sliced
2 tablespoons butter

Heat the oil in a frying pan and fry the onions, garlic and peppers for 5 minutes. Turn into a deep casserole with the courgettes (zucchini), aubergines (eggplants), mushrooms, tomatoes, tomato purée, herbs and seasoning. Pour in the stock or water. Top with the potatoes, dot with the butter and cover. Bake in a moderate oven, 180°C, 350°F, Gas Mark 4 for 1½ hours. Remove the lid and bake for 30 minutes uncovered to brown the potatoes. **Serves 4**

Cabbage and Tomato Casserole

This is a very good way of using up 'leftover' cabbage.

METRIC/IMPERIAL	AMERICAN
50 g./2 oz. butter	*¼ cup butter*
1 medium-sized onion, finely chopped	*1 medium-sized onion, finely chopped*
1 small cooking apple, peeled, cored and grated	*1 small cooking apple, peeled, cored and grated*
4 large tomatoes, peeled and chopped	*4 large tomatoes, peeled and chopped*
½ cooked, shredded cabbage	*½ cooked, shredded cabbage*
1 tablespoon chopped parsley	*1 tablespoon chopped parsley*
salt and pepper	*salt and pepper*
75 g./3 oz. Cheddar cheese, grated	*¾ cup grated Cheddar cheese*
50 g./2 oz. fresh white breadcrumbs	*1 cup fresh white breadcrumbs*

Melt the butter in a saucepan and gently fry the onion and apple for 5 minutes. Add the tomatoes and cook for a further 5 minutes, then add the cabbage, parsley and seasoning and mix well. Turn into an ovenproof dish and sprinkle with the cheese, mixed with the breadcrumbs. Cook, uncovered, in a moderately hot oven, 200°C, 400°F, Gas Mark 6 for 30 minutes or until the top is golden brown.

Serves 4 as a side dish

Savoury Stuffed Marrow (Squash)

METRIC/IMPERIAL	AMERICAN
1 medium-sized vegetable marrow	*1 medium-sized summer squash*
15 g./½ oz. butter	*1 tablespoon butter*
200 g./8 oz. minced beef	*8 oz. ground beef*
100 g./4 oz. pork sausage meat	*4 oz. pork sausage meat*
25 g./1 oz. fresh white breadcrumbs	*½ cup fresh white breadcrumbs*
1 small onion, grated	*1 small onion, grated*
1 tablespoon chopped parsley	*1 tablespoon chopped parsley*
1 tablespoon chopped chives	*1 tablespoon chopped chives*
1 teaspoon Worcestershire sauce	*1 teaspoon Worcestershire sauce*
salt and freshly ground black pepper	*salt and freshly ground black pepper*
1 egg, beaten	*1 egg, beaten*
For the sauce;	For the sauce:
25 g./1 oz. butter	*2 tablespoons butter*
25 g./1 oz. flour	*¼ cup flour*
250 ml./½ pint milk	*1¼ cups milk*
100 g./4 oz. Cheddar cheese, grated	*1 cup grated Cheddar cheese*
salt and pepper	*salt and pepper*

Peel the marrow (squash), cut it in half lengthways and scoop out the seeds. Well grease a large, shallow casserole with the butter and lay the two marrow (squash) halves in it side by side. Mix all the remaining ingredients together and use this mixture to stuff both the marrow (squash) halves. Cover and bake in a moderate oven, 180°C, 350°F, Gas Mark 4 for 1 hour.

Melt the butter for the sauce in a small pan. Add the flour and cook, stirring, for 1 minute. Gradually stir in the milk and bring to the boil, stirring all the time, until the sauce thickens. Add the cheese and season to taste with salt and pepper. Remove the lid of the casserole, strain off about half of the liquid in the casserole and pour the cheese sauce over the top. Bake for a further 20 minutes uncovered or until the sauce topping is golden brown.

Serves 4 to 6

Sauerkraut with Knackwurst

METRIC/IMPERIAL
1 large cooking apple, peeled, cored and grated
2 carrots, grated
25 g./1 oz. butter, melted
400 g./1 lb. sauerkraut
1 teaspoon caraway seeds
freshly ground black pepper
4 thick streaky or lean flank bacon rashers
4 knackwurst sausages or 8 frankfurters

AMERICAN
1 large cooking apple, peeled, cored and grated
2 carrots, grated
2 tablespoons butter, melted
1 lb. sauerkraut
1 teaspoon caraway seeds
freshly ground black pepper
4 thick fatty or lean flank bacon slices
4 knackwurst sausages or 8 frankfurters

Mix the apple, carrots, butter, sauerkraut, caraway seeds and pepper together and turn into a casserole. Top with the slices of bacon. Cover and bake in a moderately hot oven, 190°C, 375°F, Gas Mark 5 for 45 minutes. Lay the knackwurst or frankfurters on top and bake uncovered for a further 15 minutes. **Serves 4**

Outlaw Cabbage

METRIC/IMPERIAL
400 g./1 lb. cooked beef, minced
250 ml./½ pint milk
99 g./3½ oz. packet bread sauce mix
1 tablespoon tomato purée
pinch of dried mixed herbs
1 medium-sized cabbage, shredded
salt and pepper
25 g./1 oz. butter

AMERICAN
1 lb. cooked beef, ground
1¼ cups milk
3½ oz. envelope bread sauce mix
1 tablespoon tomato purée
pinch of dried mixed herbs
1 medium-sized cabbage, shredded
salt and pepper
2 tablespoons butter

Put the beef into a mixing bowl. Blend the milk with the bread sauce mix and add to the beef with the tomato purée and herbs. Mix thoroughly and turn into an ovenproof dish. Cover and bake for 25 minutes in a moderate oven, 180°C, 350°F, Gas Mark 4.

Cook the cabbage in boiling, salted water for 5 minutes. Drain, return to the pan and toss lightly with the butter and freshly ground black pepper. Spread over the meat in the dish and bake, uncovered, for a further 10 minutes. **Serves 4 to 6**

Note: *Dry bread sauce mix is used here, but if you prefer you can use 50 g./2 oz. (1 cup) fresh white breadcrumbs.*

Courgettes (Zucchini) with Parsley

METRIC/IMPERIAL
800 g./2 lb. courgettes, thinly sliced
1 teaspoon salt
50 g./2 oz. butter
freshly ground black pepper
1 tablespoon lemon juice
2 tablespoons chopped parsley

AMERICAN
2 lb. zucchini, thinly sliced
1 teaspoon salt
¼ cup butter
freshly ground black pepper
1 tablespoon lemon juice
2 tablespoons chopped parsley

Put the courgettes (zucchini) into a colander. Sprinkle with the salt and leave to drain for 30 minutes, then dry well. Well grease a casserole with some of the butter. Put about a quarter of the courgettes (zucchini) into the casserole, dot with a quarter of the remaining butter and plenty of black pepper, and repeat these layers until all the courgettes (zucchini) and butter have been used. Cover and cook in a moderate oven, 180°C, 350°F, Gas Mark 4 for 1 hour. Remove the casserole from the oven, sprinkle with the lemon juice and parsley and toss lightly together. **Serves 4 to 6 as a side dish**

Cheese, Potato and Onion Casserole

METRIC/IMPERIAL
1 large onion, thinly sliced
600 g./1½ lb. potatoes, thinly sliced
200 g./8 oz. Cheddar or Edam cheese, grated
2 tablespoons chopped parsley
salt and freshly ground black pepper
125 ml./¼ pint milk

AMERICAN
1 large onion, thinly sliced
1½ lb. potatoes, thinly sliced
2 cups grated Cheddar or Edam cheese
2 tablespoons chopped parsley
salt and freshly ground black pepper
⅝ cup milk

Put a layer of onion in a casserole, cover with a layer of potatoes and sprinkle with some of the cheese, parsley and seasoning. Repeat these layers ending with a layer of cheese. Pour over the milk, cover and bake in a moderate oven, 180°C, 350°F, Gas Mark 4 for 1¾ hours. Remove the lid of the casserole and bake for a further 15 minutes to allow the cheese and potatoes to become golden brown. **Serves 4**

Spinach Stuffed Tomatoes

METRIC/IMPERIAL
6 large tomatoes
400 g./1 lb. spinach
salt and pepper
50 g./2 oz. butter
2 to 3 tablespoons pine nuts
2 garlic cloves, crushed

AMERICAN
6 large tomatoes
1 lb. spinach
salt and pepper
¼ cup butter
2 to 3 tablespoons pine nuts
2 garlic cloves, crushed

Cut off the tops from the tomatoes and scoop out the pulp. This can be kept to use as a flavouring for another casserole or soup. Turn the tomatoes upside down on a plate or board and leave to drain while preparing the spinach.

Wash the spinach and remove any coarse stalks. Bring to the boil ¾ cm./¼ in. water in a pan with a teaspoon of salt. Add the spinach and cook for 7 to 10 minutes or until just tender. Drain well and either chop finely or blend in a liquidizer to a smooth purée. Melt the butter in a small pan and fry the pine nuts and garlic for 2 to 3 minutes. Add to the spinach, mix well and season to taste. Spoon the spinach mixture into the tomato cases and stand in a small shallow casserole. Cover and cook in a moderate oven, 180°C, 350°F, Gas Mark 4 for 20 to 30 minutes or until the tomatoes are heated through, but not too soft.

Serves 6

Note: *Do not deep freeze this dish.*

Savoury Stuffed Mushrooms

METRIC/IMPERIAL
8 large mushrooms
2 to 3 tomatoes, peeled and chopped
1 small onion, grated
40 g./1½ oz. softened butter
1 tablespoon chopped parsley
½ teaspoon chopped fresh thyme
salt and pepper

AMERICAN
8 large mushrooms
2 to 3 tomatoes, peeled and chopped
1 small onion, grated
3 tablespoons softened butter
1 tablespoon chopped parsley
½ teaspoon chopped fresh thyme
salt and pepper

Remove the stalks from the mushrooms and chop finely. Mix together with the tomatoes, onion, 25 g./1 oz. (2 tablespoons) of the softened butter, the parsley, thyme and seasoning and blend well. Place the mushroom caps on a large, lightly greased, shallow ovenproof dish or plate. Divide the stuffing between them and dot with the remaining butter. Cover and cook in a moderate oven, 180°C, 350°F, Gas Mark 4 for 20 to 30 minutes.

Serves 4 as a side dish

Note: *Do not deep freeze this dish.*

Oven-cooked Risotto

METRIC/IMPERIAL
200 g./8 oz. long grain rice
300 to 400 g./12 oz. to 1 lb. meat (see right), chopped
2 onions, sliced
200 g./8 oz. frozen mixed vegetables
1 teaspoon curry powder
1 tablespoon soy sauce
salt and pepper
500 ml./1 pint water
100 g./4 oz. Cheddar cheese, grated

AMERICAN
1⅓ cups long grain rice
12 oz. to 1 lb. meat (see right), chopped
2 onions, sliced
8 oz. frozen mixed vegetables
1 teaspoon curry powder
1 tablespoon soy sauce
salt and pepper
2½ cups water
1 cup grated Cheddar cheese

Put the rice, meat, onions and mixed vegetables into a casserole and mix together. Put the curry powder, soy sauce and seasoning into a measuring jug and add the water. Stir well, then stir into the rice mixture in the casserole. Cover and cook in a moderate oven, 180°C, 350°F, Gas Mark 4 for 1½ hours. Serve sprinkled with the grated cheese. **Serves 4**

Note: *You can use any meat you like, so long as it will be tender in 1½ hours. It is an excellent way of using up leftover cooked meat, such as lamb and pork, or it is very good with sausages, frankfurters, or tinned pork luncheon meat.*

Sausage and Red Cabbage Casserole

METRIC/IMPERIAL
400 g./1 lb. red cabbage, finely shredded
1 large onion, sliced
4 tablespoons cider or distilled malt vinegar
1 tablespoon Demerara sugar
25 g./1 oz. butter
400 g./1 lb. pork sausages
200 g./8 oz. cooking apples, peeled and chopped
1 to 2 tablespoons sultanas (optional)
125 ml./¼ pint stock
grated rind of 1 small orange
1 bay leaf
¼ teaspoon grated nutmeg
salt and pepper

AMERICAN
1 lb. red cabbage, finely shredded
1 large onion, sliced
4 tablespoons cider or distilled malt vinegar
1 tablespoon light brown sugar
2 tablespoons butter
1 lb. pork sausages
8 oz. cooking apples, peeled and chopped
1 to 2 tablespoons seedless raisins (optional)
⅝ cup stock
grated rind of 1 small orange
1 bay leaf
¼ teaspoon grated nutmeg
salt and pepper

Put the cabbage into a casserole with the onion. Mix together the vinegar and sugar and pour over the cabbage. Heat the butter in a frying pan and fry the sausages gently until golden brown. Set the sausages aside and pour the fat over the cabbage. Add the apples, sultanas (raisins), stock, grated orange rind, bay leaf, nutmeg and seasoning to the cabbage in the casserole. Mix well. Cover and cook in a moderate oven, 180°C, 350°F, Gas Mark 4 for 1 hour. Taste and adjust the seasoning, lay the sausages on top and continue cooking, covered, for a further 30 minutes. **Serves 4**

Dolmades

METRIC/IMPERIAL
425 g./15 oz. can vine leaves
3 tablespoons oil, preferably olive
2 medium-sized onions, sliced
1 garlic clove, crushed (optional)
400 g./1 lb. lean cooked beef or lamb, minced
1 tablespoon chopped parsley
4 tablespoons cooked long grain rice
2 tablespoons tomato purée
juice of 1 lemon
salt and pepper
4 tablespoons water

AMERICAN
15 oz. can vine leaves
3 tablespoons oil, preferably olive
2 medium-sized onions, sliced
1 garlic clove, crushed (optional)
1 lb. lean cooked beef or lamb, ground
1 tablespoon chopped parsley
4 tablespoons cooked long grain rice
2 tablespoons tomato purée
juice of 1 lemon
salt and pepper
4 tablespoons water

Drain the vine leaves and soak in boiling water for 1 to 2 minutes. Drain well in a colander and leave to dry while preparing the stuffing. The vine leaves are very delicate so you must take care that they do not break and tear during this process.

Heat 2 tablespoons of the oil in a pan, add the onions and garlic, if using, and fry for 5 minutes. Add the meat, parsley, rice and half the tomato purée. Continue cooking gently for a further 5 minutes. Remove from the heat, stir in the lemon juice and season to taste. Lay the vine leaves out flat on a board and put a tablespoon of the stuffing on each leaf. Roll up, tucking in the sides to make a neat roll. Arrange the rolls in a casserole. Mix the remaining tomato purée and oil with the water and pour over the rolls. Cover and cook in a moderate oven, 180°C, 350°F, Gas Mark 4 for 45 minutes. **Serves 4**

Boston Baked Beans

This is a traditional American recipe.

METRIC/IMPERIAL
600 g./1½ lb. haricot beans, soaked overnight and drained
salt and pepper
800 g./2 lb. belly pork
2 tablespoons black treacle or molasses
2 teaspoons dry mustard
2 onions, finely chopped

AMERICAN
1½ lb. haricot (dried white) beans, soaked overnight and drained
salt and pepper
2 lb. salt pork
2 tablespoons black treacle or molasses
2 teaspoons dry mustard
2 onions, finely chopped

Put the beans into a pan with fresh cold water to cover and a little salt and bring to the boil. Cover and simmer gently for 1 hour. Drain and reserve the liquid.

Score the rind of the pork, and cut the pork into two pieces. Place one piece at the bottom of a large casserole. Add the beans and bury the remainder of the pork in the beans so that the rind just shows. Stir the treacle or molasses, mustard, onions and pepper into the reserved liquid from the beans and pour over the beans in the casserole. Add more water if necessary to cover the beans. Cover the casserole and cook in a cool oven, 150°C, 300°F, Gas Mark 2 for 3 hours. Check the casserole from time to time to make sure the beans are still quite moist, and if necessary add a little extra boiling water.

Remove the lid from the casserole, bring the pork to the surface and cook uncovered for 1 hour to crisp the rind of the pork.

Serves 4 to 6

Oven-cooked Carrots

METRIC/IMPERIAL
400 g./1 lb. carrots, thinly sliced
4 tablespoons water
25 g./1 oz. butter
pinch of sugar
salt and pepper
1 tablespoon chopped parsley

AMERICAN
1 lb. carrots, thinly sliced
4 tablespoons water
2 tablespoons butter
pinch of sugar
salt and pepper
1 tablespoon chopped parsley

Put the carrots into a casserole with the water, butter, sugar and seasoning. Cover tightly and cook in a moderate oven, 180°C, 350°F, Gas Mark 4 for 1½ hours or until the carrots are tender. Serve sprinkled with the parsley.

Serves 4 as a side dish

Fruit Casseroles

These are some of the simplest of all sweet dishes to prepare and most of the recipes given in this chapter have a slightly unusual flavour variation, such as Gooseberries in Ginger Beer. For many of these recipes you can either use fresh fruit when it is cheap and in season or you can use frozen fruit. Packs of unsweetened fruit, such as rhubarb, gooseberries and plums, can be bought from freezer centres and these are particularly good for using in these dishes.

Most fruit casseroles are just as good served hot or cold, so in some cases you may feel that you want to double the quantities so that you can serve it hot one day and cold the next. If you do not want to go to the expense of serving fresh cream, remember that ice cream goes just as well with hot cooked fruit as it does with cold – in fact I think it is nicer!

Fruit that is cooked in the oven should not be cooked at a temperature higher than 170°C, 325°F, Gas Mark 3 as it tends to break up and become over-cooked. This is the temperature I have given for most of the recipes. If you are cooking something else in the oven at a lower temperature, allow a slightly longer cooking time for the fruit casserole.

Dried Apricots with Almonds

METRIC/IMPERIAL	AMERICAN
200 g./8 oz. dried apricots	*8 oz. dried apricots*
375 ml./¾ pint water	*2 cups water*
50 g./2 oz. sugar	*¼ cup sugar*
1 vanilla pod or few drops vanilla essence	*1 vanilla pod or few drops vanilla extract*
50 g./2 oz. blanched split almonds	*¼ cup blanched split almonds*

Put the dried apricots into a small casserole with the water and leave to soak for 1 hour. Add the sugar and the vanilla pod or vanilla essence (extract). Cover the casserole and cook in a cool oven, 150°C, 300°F, Gas Mark 2 for 1¾ hours. Add the almonds and cook for a further 15 minutes. Remove the vanilla pod before serving. Serve either hot or cold. **Serves 4**

Plums with Port

METRIC/IMPERIAL	AMERICAN
800 g./2 lb. plums	*2 lb. plums*
100 g./4 oz. brown sugar	*⅔ cup brown sugar*
125 ml./¼ pint port wine	*⅝ cup port wine*

Cut the plums in half and take out the stones. Put into a casserole, sprinkle over the sugar and pour the port over the top. Cover and cook in a cool oven, 150°C, 300°F, Gas Mark 2 for 45 minutes to 1 hour, or until the plums are tender.

This dish can be served hot, but is even more delicious if it is served lightly chilled with whipped cream. **Serves 4 to 6**

Baked Apples with Cider

METRIC/IMPERIAL	AMERICAN
4 eating apples	*4 eating apples*
2 tablespoons dried mixed fruit	*2 tablespoons dried mixed fruit*
2 tablespoons golden syrup	*2 tablespoons light corn syrup*
250 ml./½ pint sweet cider	*1¼ cups sweet cider*

Peel and core the apples, but leave them whole. Mix the dried fruit with the golden (light corn) syrup, then use this mixture to stuff the centre of each apple. Place in a small casserole pour over the cider and cover. Cook in a warm oven, 170°C 325°F, Gas Mark 3 for 1 hour. Serve either hot or cold.
Serves 4

Rhubarb with Orange and Honey

METRIC/IMPERIAL

600 g./1½ lb. rhubarb
grated rind and juice of 1 large orange
4 tablespoons clear honey

AMERICAN

1½ lb. rhubarb
grated rind and juice of 1 large orange
4 tablespoons clear honey

Wipe the rhubarb with a clean cloth, trim off the ends and cut into 2½ cm./1 in. pieces. Put into a casserole with the orange rind and juice and the honey. Cover and cook in a warm oven, 170°C, 325°F, Gas Mark 3 for 45 minutes to 1 hour, or until the rhubarb is tender. **Serves 4**

Bananas with Oranges

METRIC/IMPERIAL

50 g./2 oz. butter
2 tablespoons soft brown sugar
finely grated rind and juice of 1 orange
juice of ½ lemon
pinch of ground mixed spice
4 large bananas
2 tablespoons desiccated coconut

AMERICAN

¼ cup butter
2 tablespoons soft brown sugar
finely grated rind and juice of 1 orange
juice of ½ lemon
pinch of ground allspice
4 large bananas
2 tablespoons shredded coconut

Melt the butter in a pan with the brown sugar, orange rind and juice, lemon juice and mixed spice. Peel the bananas, split them in half lengthways and place in a casserole. Pour over the butter mixture, sprinkle with the coconut and bake in a moderate oven, 180°C, 350°F, Gas Mark 4 for 30 minutes. Serve hot or cold. **Serves 4**

Gooseberries in Ginger (Root) Beer

METRIC/IMPERIAL

600 g./1½ lb. gooseberries
50 to 100 g./2 to 4 oz. sugar
250 ml./½ pint ginger beer
25 g./1 oz. crystallized ginger, finely chopped

AMERICAN

1½ lb. gooseberries
¼ to ½ cup sugar
1¼ cups root beer
⅓ cup finely chopped crystallized ginger

Top and tail the gooseberries and place in a casserole.Sprinkle with the sugar; the amount of sugar required will depend on the type of gooseberries and the time of year. Pour over the ginger (root) beer. Cover the casserole and cook in a warm oven, 170°C, 325°F, Gas Mark 3 for 45 minutes to 1 hour or until the gooseberries are tender. Sprinkle with the crystallized ginger before serving. **Serves 4**

Casseroled Pears with Prunes

METRIC/IMPERIAL

200 g./8 oz. prunes
250 ml./½ pint wine or cider
400 g./1 lb. small pears, peeled, cored and quartered
grated rind and juice of 1 orange
100 g./4 oz. sugar

AMERICAN

8 oz. prunes
1¼ cups wine or cider
1 lb. small pears, peeled, cored and quartered
grated rind and juice of 1 orange
½ cup sugar

Soak the prunes overnight or for several hours in the wine or cider in a casserole. Add the pears to the casserole with the grated orange rind and juice and the sugar. Cover and cook in a warm oven, 170°C, 325°F, Gas Mark 3 for 1 hour or until the pears and prunes are quite tender. Either serve hot or allow to become cold and then chill. Serve with cream. **Serves 4 to 6**

Plum Crunch

METRIC/IMPERIAL

800 g./2 lb. plums
100 g./4 oz. Demerara sugar
50 g./2 oz. Rice Krispies or cornflakes, lightly crushed

AMERICAN

2 lb. plums
⅔ cup light brown sugar
1½ cups Rice Krispies or cornflakes, lightly crushed

Cut the plums in half and remove the stones. Place in a shallow casserole and sprinkle with the sugar mixed with the crushed Rice Krispies or cornflakes. Bake in a moderately hot oven, 190°C, 375°F, Gas Mark 5 for 45 minutes. Serve with cream.
Serves 4 to 6

Apples and Pears in Red Wine

METRIC/IMPERIAL	AMERICAN
75 g./3 oz. sugar	*3/8 cup sugar*
250 ml./1/2 pint water	*1 1/4 cups water*
250 ml./1/2 pint red wine	*1 1/4 cups red wine*
1/4 teaspoon ground cinnamon	*1/4 teaspoon ground cinnamon*
2 tablespoons redcurrant jelly	*2 tablespoons redcurrant jelly*
4 dessert pears	*4 dessert pears*
4 dessert apples	*4 dessert apples*

Put the sugar, water, wine, cinnamon and redcurrant jelly into a flameproof casserole and heat gently until the sugar and jelly have dissolved. Peel the pears, but leave whole with the stalk intact. Add to the casserole, cover and cook in a warm oven, 170°C, 325°F, Gas Mark 3 for 20 minutes. Prepare the apples in the same way as the pears and add to the casserole. Cook for 20 minutes longer.

Take the apples and pears out of the casserole and place in a serving dish. Boil the cooking liquid rapidly until it is reduced to a thin syrup. Pour over the fruit, allow to cool and then chill.

Serves 4

Apple Bake

METRIC/IMPERIAL
800 g./2 lb. cooking apples, peeled, cored and sliced
2 tablespoons water
100 g./4 oz. Demerara sugar
50 g./2 oz. cornflakes
2 tablespoons desiccated coconut
finely grated rind of 1 lemon
25 g./1 oz. butter

AMERICAN
2 lb. cooking apples, peeled, cored and sliced
2 tablespoons water
2/3 cup light brown sugar
1 cup cornflakes
2 tablespoons shredded coconut
finely grated rind of 1 lemon
2 tablespoons butter

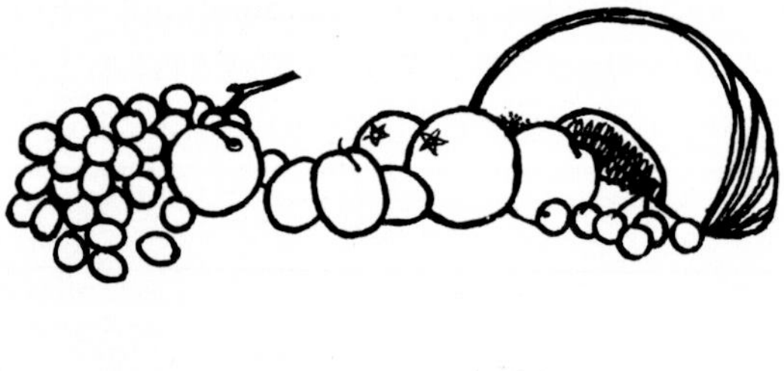

Put the apples into a saucepan with the water and half the sugar. Cover and cook over a gentle heat until the apples are soft. Either turn into four individual ovenproof dishes or one large one. Mix together the cornflakes, coconut, remaining sugar and lemon rind. Sprinkle over the apples. Dot with the butter. Bake the small individual dishes in a moderately hot oven, 170°C, 375°F, Gas Mark 5 for 20 minutes or the large dish for 40 minutes. **Serves 4**

Dried Fruit and Nut Salad

METRIC/IMPERIAL
100 g./4 oz. prunes
100 g./4 oz. dried apricots
100 g./4 oz. dried figs
50 g./2 oz. raisins
750 ml./1½ pints water
25 g./1 oz. shelled walnuts
25 g./1 oz. blanched almonds
25 g./1 oz. pine nuts (optional)

AMERICAN
⅔ cup prunes
⅔ cup dried apricots
⅔ cup dried figs
⅓ cup raisins
3¾ cups water
3 tablespoons shelled walnuts
3 tablespoons blanched almonds
3 tablespoons pine nuts (optional)

Put the prunes, apricots, figs and raisins into a casserole. Add the water and leave to soak overnight. Cover and cook in a cool oven, 150°C, 300°F, Gas Mark 2 for 1 hour. Add the nuts. Allow to cool, and then chill. **Serves 6 to 8**

Cherry Compôte

METRIC/IMPERIAL
600 g./1½ lb. dark red cherries, stoned
6 tablespoons red wine
3 tablespoons redcurrant jelly
1 tablespoon sugar
finely grated rind and juice of 1 orange
pinch of ground cinnamon

AMERICAN
1½ lb. dark red cherries, pitted
6 tablespoons red wine
3 tablespoons redcurrant jelly
1 tablespoon sugar
finely grated rind and juice of 1 orange
pinch of ground cinnamon

Put the cherries in a casserole with the wine, redcurrant jelly, sugar, orange rind and juice and cinnamon. Cover and cook in a warm oven, 170°C, 325°F, Gas Mark 3 for 35 minutes. Allow to cool, then chill lightly before serving. **Serves 6**

Note: *If you prefer the syrup lightly thickened you can blend a teaspoon of arrowroot with the strained syrup. Bring to the boil in a small saucepan, then add the cooked cherries, cool and chill as above.*

Index

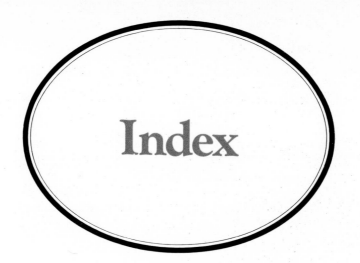

Acknowledgments

The publishers gratefully acknowledge the use of photographs from the following sources:
Argentine Beef Bureau 8; Bryce Attwell 89; California Prune Advisory Bureau 12; Colman's Mustard 13; Eden Vale Ltd 72; Electricity Council 71; Flour Advisory Bureau 82; Fruit Producers' Council 51, 76, 123; Herring Industry Board 97; John West Foods Ltd 56, 98, 99; Kellogg Co of Great Britain 124; Knorr 24–25; Lawry's Foods Inc 11, 17; Lea & Perrins Worcestershire Sauce 18–19; Michael Leale 14, 27, 73, 74, 79, 93; John Lee 31, 42–43, 53, 108, 111, 115; National Dairy Council 61; National Magazine Co Ltd 45, 63, 72; *New Idea* Magazine 9; New Zealand Lamb Information Bureau 38–39, 41; Norman Nicholls 23, 30, 34, 35, 36, 37, 40, 60, 70, 83, 92, 95, 101, 104, 105, 106, 109, 113, 114, 117, 119, 125, 126; Olives from Spain 21, 50; Pentangle Photography 77; Roger Phillips 2–3, 6, 29, 33, 46, 58, 67, 68–69, 85, 90–91, 102–103, 120–121; RHM Foods 55; Sausage Advisory Bureau 107; Taunton Cider 48–49; U.S. Rice Council 81.